Rapid READING

The high-speed way to increase your learning power

Geoffrey A. Dudley

Thorsons
An Imprint of HarperCollinsPublishers

Thorsons
An Imprint of HarperCollins*Publishers*
77–85 Fulham Palace Road,
Hammersmith, London W6 8JB
1160 Battery Street,
San Francisco, California 94111–1213

First published by Thorsons 1977
This edition 1995
3 5 7 9 10 8 6 4 2

A catalogue record for this book
is available from the British Library

ISBN 0 7225 3154 0

Printed and bound in Great Britain by
Caledonian International Book Manufacturing Ltd, Glasgow

CONTENTS

To Nichola, Darren, Jonathan and Michael

HOW TO READ THIS BOOK

Start by reading the instructions on this and the next page. They serve as an introduction to the chapters that follow. Then go to Chapter 1. Read it carefully, pausing to think over its points and to carry out its recommendations. Next answer the self-testing quiz. Check your answers against the answer key. The answer keys for all the self-testing quizzes will be found at the end of the book. Afterwards proceed to the next chapter; and so on, following the same procedure throughout.

Some of the selections require you to time yourself as you read them. The following simple procedure is suggested for doing this. Of course, if you have a stop-watch you can use it, but these instructions assume that you will be using an ordinary watch with a second-hand.

How to time your reading
1. Write down what the exact time will be when the second-hand of your watch reaches the 60 figure.
2. Commence to read at that point.
3. As soon as you finish reading write down the exact time in minutes and seconds.
4. You can convert your time into a reading speed by dividing the length of the extract (in words) by your reading time (in seconds) and multiplying the answer by 60. This gives you your reading time in words per minute. For example, suppose you read an extract of 1,000 words in 2 minutes 20 seconds. Converting this time to seconds gives 140 seconds.

We then divide 1,000 by 140 and multiply the result by 60, as follows:

$$\frac{1,000}{140} \times \frac{60}{1} = \frac{3,000}{7}$$

$$= 429 \text{ approx.}$$

Your reading speed, then, is 429 words per minute for this particular extract.

Finally, when you have finished the book remember to apply what you have learned to your ordinary everyday reading. Whether it is business or official correspondence, textbooks for examination purposes, or light reading of novels for relaxation, the principles taught in these chapters will serve you well and help you to read material of any kind rapidly and with comprehension.

CHAPTER ONE

WHY READ FASTER?

You have picked up this book because you want to be able to read faster. You hope to gain the benefits which rapid reading can bring to your business and social life. What these benefits are I will reveal in a moment, but first let me welcome you as a reader. I know that I can rely on you to put your best efforts into this cause.

The aim of the book is indeed to help you to read faster. I want to assist you to accomplish the reading goal which you have set for yourself. I hope, in fact, that as you work through the chapters you will find that your reading ambitions have been too modest, and that you can accomplish much more than you expected at first.

The first thing to do is to remind yourself what you demand from these chapters. What, then, are the benefits to be gained from faster reading?

How rapid reading helps you

1. *Rapid reading saves time.* This is the most obvious benefit. Do you find yourself finishing the Sunday paper in the middle of the week? Or reading the morning or evening daily paper when it is already a day old? Do you find time to read the magazines that are delivered to you weekly or monthly?

Rapid reading enables you to avoid constantly having to renew your library books because you have been unable to read them in the time allowed, or being tempted to keep them beyond the allotted time and having to pay a fine when you do eventually return them.

By reading faster you gain extra hours which can be devoted either to extra reading or to something else which appeals to you. Most of us complain that we haven't enough time to do all the interesting things which we would like to do. If you have ever voiced this complaint and if you are in the habit of doing much reading, you can congratulate yourself that you have found in this book a simple means of getting through your reading quicker.

2. *Rapid reading makes for greater efficiency.* Getting through your reading faster makes you better able to cope with the demands of modern business. To become a faster reader will mean that you are a more efficient worker, and this will smooth the path of your advancement in the business world. This is because people who read faster also understand better. They grasp more readily the meaning and implications of what they read. Consequently they are able to make more effective use of the time they spend on reading, and this reflects credit on themselves and promotes smoother working generally. To read faster, then, will make you a more valuable employee.

Rapid reading has specific occupational value to those whose work mainly consists in reading, e.g. publishers' readers, research workers, students, abstractors, etc.

3. *The less time spent on routine matters, the more time available for policy-making.* If you are an employer or an executive you are bound to have a lot of paper work each day. The quicker you can deal with it, the more time you can devote to the essential activities of policy-making. To learn the art of rapid reading prevents you from getting bogged down in the mass of letters, memoranda and reports that seem inseparable from professional work.

4. *Rapid reading has entertainment value.* The value of faster reading is not confined to work. It also increases your enjoyment of sports and entertainments where reading is necessary. For example, do you go to foreign films? Can you read the subtitles fast enough not to let them distract your attention from the action on the screen? Do you read novels? The more novels you can get through the more advantageous use you can make of your library. These are just two typical ways in which faster reading can benefit you in the sphere of

entertainment and leisure activities.

5. *Rapid reading broadens your mental horizon.* It broadens your mental horizon by putting within your reach a greater range or variety of reading matter.

6. *Rapid reading helps effective speaking.* It enables you to gather more speedily the material you need for public speaking or conversation.

7. *Rapid reading helps you to pass examinations.* If you are studying for an examination it allows you to get through your syllabus with greater ease.

8. *Rapid reading improves your understanding.* It has been shown that rapid readers also grasp more quickly what they read. The claim has been made that 'every adult of normal intelligence who struggles along at less than 300 words per minute is reading at a slower rate than his ability to comprehend requires.'

9. *Rapid reading keeps you up to date.* It enables you to keep abreast of the news and of the latest developments in your own particular field.

10. *Rapid reading is a mental tonic.* It acts as a general mental tonic, brushing up your knowledge, exercising your intellect and keeping you mentally on your toes.

Speed and comprehension

'A page digested,' wrote Macaulay, 'is better than a volume hurriedly read.' If this is true why am I setting out to teach you how to read faster?

Macaulay lived in a leisurely age in which there were both less to read and more time to read it. In the age of speed and progress in which we live efficiency depends to a quite unprecedented extent on how rapidly we can read.

In any case, as I hope to show, reading faster is not incompatible with digesting what is read. Just because we read at a higher rate than Macaulay thought proper it does not mean that we are reading superficially. Not at all. The aim is to read with both speed and comprehension.

Even Macaulay would no doubt have admitted that two pages read and digested are better than one page read and digested in the same time. This is the goal to keep before you in this book. The reader can, in fact, look forward to an improvement of 100 per cent or even more in both his speed of reading and his understanding of the material which he reads.

Mastering the subject

I wish to avoid the difficulty experienced by a man who reported: 'Whenever I read at a rate faster than usual I am at a loss to grasp the meaning which the author is trying to convey. I have tried all methods to overcome this difficulty, such as memorising key paragraphs, etc., but it has been of no use. This usually results in my giving up the study of a subject, even though at the start I may have been deeply interested in it.'

Nevertheless it is true that to be interested in what you are reading helps you to read it rapidly. A lady reader said: 'I read on at great speed because the book is interesting. I find that when I get to the bottom of the page I have a good idea of what I have read.'

Even if one does experience some difficulty in understanding what is read rapidly, a page can probably be mastered better by reading it rapidly several times than by reading it slowly once.

That to read slowly does not necessarily mean that we grasp better is clearly illustrated by the following reported experience: 'I have decided to take up a correspondence course. One of the things I need urgently in my studies is to know how to improve my memory and how to assimilate new interesting subjects. *I am a very slow reader* and I should like to be able to grasp the main theme of any subject.'

A point to note, however, is that, although reading and rereading is the commonest method of study, it isn't the best. A more efficient way is to read and then test yourself after closing the book, e.g., by asking yourself questions about what you have read, by discussing it with someone else who has read it, or by attempting to answer the author's questions. That is the method I favour your adopting in dealing with this book.

Reading and age

These words are no doubt being read by many people in the second half of life. Indeed they may be read by some who already consider themselves well advanced in years. If you fall into this category you will probably be asking yourself: Can I benefit from this training in spite of my age?

The answer, you will be pleased to know, is a reassuring yes. The undeservedly popular adage 'You can't teach an old dog new tricks' is untrue. It is not impossible for an ageing person to learn a new skill like faster reading. Of course, it may be a little more difficult than for a person of, say, half his age. Nevertheless, the ability to learn depreciates very slowly with age, provided that the will to learn is retained.

Effects of TV on reading

Another question that might be raised is: What is the point of teaching people to read faster when, owing to the influence of TV, less is being read altogether? If less is being read, people will have more time to get through it and consequently they won't need to learn to read faster.

This view appears to be based on a fallacy. It implies an assumption that isn't true. It assumes that because of TV people are, in fact, reading less. Publishers have been unable to confirm this. Indeed, what seems to have happened is that TV has awakened the interest of more people in more subjects. They have been led to seek more information which they have had to go to books to obtain. The result has been that TV has encouraged more reading rather than less.

In a letter written to *The Guardian* the librarian of a town in the south of England said that book borrowings from his library had risen by 100 per cent in the past ten years. He adds, however, the significant fact that the increased demand has been for the more serious type of book, and that it is only readers of thrillers and light fiction who have been lost to TV in recent years.

A similar experience was reported by the head of Manchester Public Libraries. He found that, while issues of light fiction dropped from 2,911,000 to 2,615,000 in the eight years following the opening of ITV in the north of England, issues of non-fiction increased from 2,460,000 to 3,681,000 in the same period. He commented: 'The correlation between the growth in the number of television sets and the decline in novel-reading is hardly coincidental.'

The problem has also been examined by a psychologist, who compared 137 TV-owning families with the same number of non-TV-owning families. Both groups were closely similar as regards the type of area where they resided and their standard of living.

He found, as we would expect, that 'leisure-time activities carried on at home suffer under the influence of TV.' His data did not, however, support the impression that reading suffers considerably in homes with TV. 'Compared to radio listening and many other entertainments,' he reports, '*reading is holding its own relatively well in our TV families.*'

Need of rapid reading widely recognized

The following cry from the heart comes from the Group Secretary of a Hospital Management Committee in the south of England: 'With the ever-increasing amount of correspondence and publications that passes through the office, it has become difficult for the average mind to retain all the information fed into it.'

The need to read faster to get through the mountains of correspondence, memoranda and documents that face the busy executive is widely recognized to-day in all quarters both high and low.

Members of the Government and Foreign Office trained themselves to read faster. So did the late President Kennedy.

Mr J.C. Garner, head of the Liberal Studies Department of the Royal College of Advanced Technology, Salford, was reported in the press as saying: 'We aim at teaching men who are already qualified technicians and business men how to read more quickly and efficiently.' He was referring to the College's course in communication by reading for business executives. 'It is possible for us,' he added, 'during our ten-week course to help men read at a rate of 500 words a minute.'

The Carborundum Co. Ltd, ICI, Leyland Motors, and Joseph Lucas are among the firms in this country who have encouraged or trained their executive staff to learn to read faster and get through their paper work in quicker time.

The Chief Proprietor of *The Times* is reported as saying that he regretted having been a slow reader. Reflecting that some of his friends, who were busier men than he, read three or four books a week, he lamented the fact that he had never acquired the skill of rapid reading. He might have quoted the example of Cecil Harmsworth King, another newspaper tycoon, who is said to read four books a week, two of them usually in French.

Rapid reading is invaluable in the Services too. There also it is essential to get through paper work with the utmost despatch so that vital military duties may not suffer. The military man rightly takes the view that national defence must not be held up by excessive time spent on bumf, as paper work is picturesquely called in the British Army.

A correspondent writing to the press tells us that at Manchester University over forty years ago Professor Septimus Lodge, brother of Sir Oliver, trained his students to read at high speed. He applied the principle not only to English but also to French, forcing his students to work through a French grammar in four weeks and in nine weeks to read French literature as fast as English.

Increasing the word span

One of the basic principles on which speed reading relies is that of increasing the word span. The word span is the number of words that are taken in on one fixation of the eyes. According to Dr Earl A. Taylor of the Reading and Study Centre in New York, the average adult's word span is 1·06 words per fixation. That is to say, he stops at practically every word. He reads slowly because he reads one word at a time.

Speed reading aims to increase the number of words taken in at a single glance. Instead of pausing at every word we can take in a phrase or a whole sentence at a glance. If we can increase our word span to, say, four or five words per glance, it is obvious that we are going to be able to enjoy a considerable increase in our speed of reading.

This point is underlined by William Schaill of Reading Laboratory Inc. 'After all,' he reminds us, 'the words "The red barn" are only a picture of a red barn. If you read it word by word you don't get any more out of it than by reading it as a phrase. You can see as many as five words in a phrase.'

Paul B. Panes of the Reading Institute of New York University even questions whether it is necessary to read every word even in a phrase. 'An efficient reader,' he affirms, 'never reads every word. He reads about 50 per cent of the words, unless the material is technical. The essential reading skill is the ability to find the main idea of a paragraph.'

To avoid missing key words is a matter of experience and training. The point is illustrated by Panes's own sentence:

An efficient reader never reads every word.

If you don't read the word *never*, you won't get the meaning of the sentence. On the other hand, you can still get the meaning even if you leave out two other words:

Efficient reader never every word.

However, suppose you overlook *never*, so that you read: 'An efficient reader reads every word.' If you do this, you won't be able to make sense of the next two sentences in the above quotation. These sentences signal to you that you have missed a key word, thus encouraging you to form the habit of picking out ideas instead of reading every word.

This is intelligent skipping. It is skimming with a definite purpose, the purpose being to get at the meaning faster.

Preliminary practice material

Now to 'blood' yourself. You must initiate yourself gently into what you intend to make habitual. Give yourself a little practice in the art of rapid reading. You need not take this too seriously for a start. You need not make hard work of the simple exercise proposed below.

All you have to do is to read the piece – but 'put on the pressure' just a little. That is, read it at a slightly faster speed than you would if you were going to work through it at your usual leisurely pace.

The purpose of this exercise is to get a foretaste, as it were, of what is to come. You want to test yourself – to convince yourself that the task you are attempting is within your powers. You want both to encourage yourself and also to prove to yourself that it is easier than it may have seemed at first.

A word of warning before you start. Do not make the mistake of trying to force yourself to read faster by an effort of will. Rather bring to your aid the power of imagination. As you tackle this piece let your imagination get to work on your behalf. Picture yourself reading just a little faster than you are accustomed to. See yourself in your mind's eye finishing this extract just a little ahead of the time that you would normally require.

If you do this you will find that the task of your will is considerably lightened. You will find that you don't have to force yourself quite as much. The task has already appealed to your imagination and you are merely aligning your will in the same direction.

So sit down and start off reading this selection. It is a news item about a railway crash. Remember what you have to do. You have to read this piece just a little faster than you would normally do, and as you attempt it you are to picture yourself in your mind's eye accomplishing the task with ease.

Ready now? Right then – off you go!

187 DIE IN HOLIDAY RAIL DISASTER
Heaviest toll for 25 years
From our own Correspondent

Seuilly-la-Reine (Northern France), Sept. 18

187 people were killed when a holiday train crowded with excursionists was involved in collision with a goods train here yesterday. This is one of the worst disasters in European railway history for 25 years. The toll also included 56 persons injured.

The accident occurred when the excursion train was halted in the station at Seuilly-la-Reine. A goods train heavily loaded

with iron ore ran into it from behind after getting out of
control on an incline immediately outside the station.

The heavy goods locomotive ploughed into the rear coaches
of the passenger train with a terrific impact, completely
shattering them. Practically all the coaches of the excursion
train were derailed and several were telescoped by the force of
the collision.

Most of the casualties were in the rear half of the train. In
the end two coaches there were no survivors, and even in the
front of the train passengers were thrown heavily on top of one
another and cut by flying glass.

Rescue workers toiled in the gathering dusk to free the
trapped and injured and to recover the bodies of the dead.
Those quickly on the scene with assistance included a
detachment of French infantry soldiers who were in camp at
the nearby village of Maisons Malfort.

The passenger train had taken excursionists on a day trip
from Paris to the Forest of Montraison, which is a well-known
beauty spot much frequented by Parisians and workers in the
northern suburbs of the capital. It had just pulled up at
Seuilly-la-Reine to discharge the handful of passengers who
had joined it there earlier in the day.

When the crash occurred many people were standing in the
corridors and were thrown with considerable force as coaches
toppled off the permanent way. The station-master at Seuilly
estimated that the goods train must have been travelling at
least 50 miles an hour when it hit the rear coaches of the
passenger train. Other eyewitnesses of the disaster confirmed
this statement and added that when the impact occurred the
momentum of the goods train carried it forward many yards,
splitting the coaches of the passenger train and tossing them
aside.

'I was standing near the front of the train,' said Jean-Paul
Belley, porter at Seuilly. 'Suddenly I saw the goods train
approaching down the incline round a bend in the rear. I
shouted to people on the train, trying to warn them of the
danger. But no one appeared to take any notice except the
people standing on the platform, who ran for safety, as
coaches were derailed around them.'

'It was terrible,' added Madeleine Verneuil, one of the passengers who had dismounted. 'The cries of the injured and dying were heart-rending as the goods train simply seemed to sweep the excursion train off the rails, brushing it from its path like so much matchwood. The whole of the rear of the train seemed to disintegrate.'

Priests hastily summoned from the surrounding villages of this part of the Ile de France moved about the wreckage saying prayers and administering the last rites to victims who were dying. Nursing sisters from the hospital of Notre Dame de la Charité in Seuilly helped to give blood transfusions to the badly injured, and doctors were at work administering injections to ease the pain of the injured as they lay trapped in the debris.

To-morrow a full inquiry into the circumstances of the accident is being opened by the prefecture of the Oise division of the gendarmerie. Meanwhile many charitable organisations in France are raising funds to relieve the distress of the families bereaved by the accident, and appeals for donations are to be made by prominent speakers on radio and TV.

Footnote to yesterday's accident. – A six-weeks-old baby girl was found uninjured in a derailed coach in the centre of the train. Her injured mother was found lying beside her. Both mother and child are receiving care in the local hospital before being sent home to Paris.

2 min 45 secs

SELF-TESTING QUIZ

Put a tick opposite the statements which you have read in Chapter 1.
1. The aim of the book is to help you to read faster.
2. By reading faster you gain extra hours.
3. You can gain advancement in the business world even without reading faster.
4. The value of faster reading is confined to work.
5. Rapid reading helps you to pass examinations.
6. Rapid readers grasp more quickly what they read.
7. You can read with speed or comprehension but not both.
8. To be interested in what you are reading does not help you to read it rapidly.

9. A page can probably be mastered better by reading it rapidly several times than by reading it slowly once.

10. Reading and rereading is both the commonest and the best method of study.

11. It is not impossible for an aging person to learn to read faster.

12. TV has had no effect on reading.

13. The Chief Proprietor of *The Times* was reported as regretting having been a slow reader.

14. The word span is the number of words that are taken in on one fixation of the eyes.

15. The average adult reads slowly because he reads one word at a time.

Now check your answers against the answer key which you will find on page 159.

CHAPTER TWO

HOW TO CONCENTRATE

Before you can learn to read faster you must first learn to concentrate. There is little point in letting your eyes skim faster over a page of print if you are not really attending to it even when you read it slowly. Understanding of what you read depends on the attention you pay to it, and without this attention comprehension cannot be increased by reading faster.

What do we mean when we speak of concentration? We have given some hint of its meaning in the foregoing paragraph. Concentration is sustained attention; it means putting oneself in the *centre* of something. This process of focusing the mind upon a task may be compared with a magnifying glass which brings to a focus the rays of the sun.

In correct concentration, says F. S. Perls, 'the object occupies the foreground of consciousness without any effort, the rest of the world disappears, time and surroundings cease to exist; no internal conflict or protest against the concentration arises.'

This writer points out that 'such concentration is easily found in children, and often in adults when they are engaged in some interesting work or hobby.' He adds that 'as every part of the personality is temporarily co-ordinated and subordinated to one purpose only, it is not difficult to realize that such an attitude is the basis of every development.'

When the mind wanders

It is certainly the basis of the reading development which you are seeking here. Its opposite is the condition of mind-wandering which you are seeking to overcome. This condition is well illustrated by the following typical case.

A young law student who complained of absent-mindedness and lack of concentration reported the following day-dreams: 'If I saw a nice car, I fancied it was mine. If I saw a nice house, it was mine, and so on. If I was sick, in day-dreams I fancied that I was never sick. When I went to college, I spent at least two hours daily day-dreaming in a quiet place, and after that I was happy; nothing ever worried me.

'I left college and found employment, but still I was dreaming of London and university life. There was no corner of London to which I had not been in day-dreams. I had a map of London and spent quiet times dreaming that I was there, my education being sponsored by a very wealthy father. Sometimes when I went to sleep, the day-dream came true in my dreams. I would be in London chatting with the sons of lords.'

Besides illustrating that day-dreams, like the dreams of sleep, are imaginary gratifications of wishes, this man's experiences illustrate the continuity that exists between day-dreams and the dreams of sleep.

They also throw interesting light on the psychology of the student himself. Glancing over the thoughts that crossed his mind as he sat idly over his books, we see distinctly that he uses day-dreaming as a means of compensating himself for an inferiority complex. He is constantly comparing himself with other people whom he considers to be more successful than he. We also notice the wish-fulfilling fantasy of life in London. These fanciful ideas and stray thoughts fill his mind so completely that he may be said to be concentrating on them instead of on his books.

Here is another example of the kinds of thoughts that are liable to occur when attempting to concentrate.

'For years,' said another young man, 'I have done a good deal of fanciful day-dreaming. At odd moments of the day, when my mind is not fixed on anything in particular, I will imagine myself scoring the winning goal in an important football match, winning at an athletics meeting or addressing a public meeting. All of these dreams are concerned with personal prestige and the desire to be appreciated. I am led to believe that these dreams are the mind's compensation for some of the things we would like but have not got, i.e., a bit of the limelight. Or are they just an attempt to escape from the realities of life?'

He himself offers the correct explanation of his habit of day-dreaming. This is, as he points out, a means of compensating in fantasy for the satisfaction he fails to achieve in reality. As he himself put it, 'These dreams are the mind's compensation for some of the things I would like but have not got.'

The task that faces him is to use his abilities so as to make some contribution to the welfare of society at large. In his book *What Life Should Mean to You* Dr Alfred Adler writes: 'A man whose love-life is an intimate and many-sided co-operation, whose work results in useful achievements, and whose contacts with his fellows are wide and fruitful ... feels life as a creative task offering many opportunities and no irrecoverable defeats.' Elsewhere he adds: 'When an individual fails to square himself with one or more of these three inexorable demands on life, beware of feelings of abasement.' The above man's habit of day-dreaming about personal prestige points to just such feelings of abasement, for which the day-dreaming is intended to console him.

In both cases above the train of thoughts gives a clue to the fact that the persons who produced them are preoccupied with the idea of compensating themselves in fantasy for the satisfaction they fail to achieve in reality. They seek to console themselves for their lost opportunities with interests developed in the realm of imagination. One detects traces of the wish to enjoy a little of the limelight that they feel has so far been denied them in life. All of these thoughts emerge to distract their attention as they sit down to read.

Disadvantages of day-dreaming
These two cases make it quite clear what the disadvantages of day-dreaming are. Four unhealthy effects of day-dreaming, according to Dr J.E. Wallace Wallin, are:

1. It encourages the individual in a tendency to escape from reality and avoid responsibility.

2. It is an illusory method of compensating for frustration and feelings of inferiority.
3. Day-dreams of the conquering hero type may lead to conceit in the individual's real-life social relations.
4. The individual's judgment may become impaired so that he fails altogether to distinguish between fantasy and reality.

Advantages of concentration

Over against these disadvantages we may set the following advantages of concentration:

1. People will enjoy your company if you can pay attention to them and their affairs.
2. To concentrate on what others are saying enables you to ask intelligent questions or make intelligent comments.
3. The ability to concentrate strengthens one's self-esteem and improves the opinion that other people have of us.
4. It enables us to accomplish the tasks that face us. Sir Isaac Newton was once asked how he came to make his great discoveries. He replied: 'I keep the subject continually before me and wait till the first dawnings open slowly, little by little, into full clear light.'
5. Concentration makes for greater accuracy. This is especially important to ensure comprehension of what we plan to read rapidly.
6. Learning to concentrate enables you not only to read faster but also to remember what you read.

Why we lack concentration

What are the causes of lack of concentration? Why do we find our attention wandering as we try to read? There are four main reasons for lack of concentration. They are:

1. Outer distractions.
2. Inner distractions.
3. Loss of interest in the subject-matter.
4. A conflict between will-power and imagination.

According to Margaret O. Hyde in *Your Brain — Master Computer* (The World's Work Ltd.), recent research also indicates that a part of the brain called the reticular formation affects concentration. It screens the many sensations reaching the brain at a given moment and selects the ones to be attended to. The reticular formation of people who cannot concentrate may not be acting efficiently, but at the present time science has developed no method of controlling this activity.

1. *Outer distractions*. These may be arranged under a number of headings according to the particular sense organ which they affect. Traditionally there are five senses: sight, hearing, smell, taste and touch. A scene outside the window, a noise in the room, the smell of fish cooking in the kitchen, the taste of a fruit drop we are sucking, and the feel of a pen that we are not used to – all these are extraneous stimuli that, impinging upon one or other of the five traditional senses, may disturb our concentration.

But the modern view is that the five mentioned above are not the only sense organs which we possess. The list of senses has been extended to include also:

> Pressure
> Temperature
> Pain
> Muscle
> Equilibrium
> Hunger
> Thirst

If the collar of our shirt is too tight-fitting our pressure sense makes us aware of the distraction. If the room is too hot or too cold the effect of this on our temperature sense may distract our attention. If we try to read in spite of a raging toothache the painful stimulus will act through our pain sense to interfere with concentration.

Distractions may also act through our muscle sense. It is this which diverts our attention to the weight of the book in our hand or to the effort of sitting upright in our chair. We become aware of distractions arising from the position of our body in space. If the chair is uncomfortable and our limbs are cramped in an awkward position our sense of equilibrium brings this to our notice.

Hunger and thirst, too, are 'outer' distractions impeding our efforts to concentrate. This usage of the word distinguishes them from distractions arising within the mind. These will be considered in the next section.

2. *Inner distractions.* These are sources of distraction which arise within the mind as distinct from those like sights and sounds which arise outside of it. Inner distractions are chiefly of two kinds. Some reference has already been made to the first kind, which is day-dreaming. The second kind is emotional conflict. Emotions like worry, fear, grief, jealousy, and so on create conflict in the mind and interfere with our ability to study. This is perhaps the strongest source of interference.

We become aware at this point of the fact that we cannot concentrate on more than one thing at a time. While we are preoccupied with our worry or grief or other disturbing emotion we cannot give our attention properly to the material which we want to learn to read faster.

A Japanese called Mr Tameo Kajiyama has claimed to be able to concentrate on more than one thing at a time. He says that this is shown by his ability to read or write upside down and backwards, carry on a conversation, and work out the cube roots to numbers all at the same time.

We might think that this is a remarkable performance. Indeed it is – but it doesn't violate the law of attention, as this principle of the 'one-track' mind is known. No, what happens in Mr Kajiyama's case is that his attention alternates rapidly backwards and forwards among a variety of tasks. Given a long enough training any normally intelligent person could probably accomplish the same feat of alternating his attention – if he thought it worth while to do so.

A bus conductor said: 'A few months ago I began to notice that I was becoming absent-minded, and of late this has increased to an embarrassing degree, so much so that I repeatedly forget and leave my things about. My absent-mindedness has caused me quite recently to make a most embarrassing error that savoured almost of dishonesty, but it was quite unconsciously committed. A few days ago a passenger asked the fare for a certain distance. I told him that it was 90p, which he paid, but in error I issued a 9p ticket. This was discovered when an inspector came on the bus to check.'

This experience illustrates how memory depends upon attention, which in turn depends upon freedom from distraction. To carry out a task efficiently or to remember something properly we have to attend to it. This man was absent-minded because he was not attending to his job. The reasons why his attention was distracted were revealed in the following remarks:

'The night before this incident a young hooligan attacked me, compelling me to defend myself. This experience upset me terribly and put me in an emotional state which preoccupied me all through the following day.'

In most cases we are safe in attributing inability to concentrate to interference by inner emotional conflicts. The incapacity to 'take in' what we are supposed to be reading is due to the intervention of repressed thoughts and emotions.

A further striking illustration of this is the case of a young man studying at college. 'Since finding myself a sweetheart last year,' he admitted, 'I cannot concentrate but am always thinking about her and the wonderful times we have together. Whenever I take up a book my mind is filled with day-dreams. No matter how much I force myself back to the work in hand, I am constantly distracted by wandering thoughts. I may have to read even simple sentences many times before their meaning sinks in. What must I do to concentrate on my reading? Can you help me to increase my speed and understanding? Otherwise I do not think I shall be able to pass my Advanced GCE Papers at the present rate of only three pages in two hours' reading.'

This admission illustrates not only the impairment of concentration by day-dreaming but also the factor of emotional conflict. His rate of reading is low because he does not concentrate; and he does not concentrate because there is a conflict of interests between his girl friend and his reading. Possibly, too, he is worried to some extent, e.g. about his future career, marriage, etc.

'It is concentration, more than any other single factor in the reading process,' says Norman Lewis of the College of the City of New York, 'which increases a person's understanding and speed.'

3. *Loss of interest in the subject-matter.* Even if the bus conductor whose case is quoted above had not had his emotional problem, attention to his job would still have been difficult, because he was not really interested in it. 'I find my job most uncongenial,' he said, 'and stick it only because my opportunities for employment are limited.'

A young woman law student was preparing to sit for her bar finals, which she had already postponed for six months. She complained of lack of concentration. 'I am not very fond of law,' she admitted, 'and I do not think I shall be good at it. I feel very self-conscious when speaking in public.'

Asked why she was training for a career in which she was not interested, she replied at first that she was doing it at the insistence of her parents, who wanted her to have a 'useful' profession. It appeared that she herself really wanted to be an interior decorator. Her parents had objected to this, however, and she had taken what she called 'the line of least resistance.'

She revealed that she had an older sister who was already practising law. 'My sister has proved her worth,' she said, 'and is greatly admired and respected by the community. I am the youngest of three sisters and so am considered the "baby" of the family and left out of grown-up affairs. I was treated as "that sweet kid" and then dismissed from their minds. *I tried to get their attention and only in that way did I succeed.* Or if I could not get my way I would start to cry. Compared with my sisters, I was very slow. *That comparison has been carried on* up till now, mainly with my eldest sister, and I cannot help but feel inferior to her. *I cannot help wishing I could be like her.* Everyone makes comparisons between us, saying that she took a shorter time over her training and asking me when mine will be finished. All these thoughts run through my mind while I am studying.'

This young woman was unable to concentrate on her studies because she was not interested in them. Nevertheless, she had a powerful motive for going in for law – quite apart from her parents' insistence on the need of a 'useful' profession. Her real motive for what she was doing was a wish to prove herself the equal of her older sister, who was already established in the legal profession. Qualifying as a lawyer was to her a means whereby she hoped to come to terms with her rivalry with her sister, and thus compensate herself for her feeling of inferiority as the youngest member of the family constellation.

Her motive for yielding to her parents' insistence was to win their attention by equalling her sister's achievement. Her complaint about her inability to concentrate served the same purpose now as her being a 'cry baby' did when she was younger.

Lack of interest in a particular thing, then – or a conflict between interests in different things – can lead to mind-wandering. Our attention drifts away from the subject in hand because interests in other things interfere with the process of single-minded absorption which is essential for concentration.

A recognised means of diverting our attention from something unpleasant, e.g. shock or grief, is, in fact, to cultivate interests different from the interest that led to the unpleasant experience. This is because, as we have seen, interests in other things interfere with the process of sustained attention upon which the focusing of the mind depends.

4. *A conflict between will-power and imagination.* Most of us have heard of the psychological law known as the law of reversed effort. This states that in a conflict between will and imagination the latter proves the stronger.

Such a conflict may be exemplified by our attitude towards the task of concentrating upon a piece of reading. We try to succeed at the task by an effort of will. At the same time we let our imagination dwell on the pleasure of not doing the reading at all or of doing something else which perhaps at the moment appeals to us more strongly.

In this conflict imagination proves the stronger. The result is that our mind wanders away from the task in hand. The law of reversed effort furnishes yet another reason for lack of concentration.

For example, a man said: 'I sit down at my books intent on doing an evening's study. But as soon as I open a book I think of something else that I would sooner be doing. I try to bring my mind back by the use of will-power, but the effort proves too much for my weak will. Thoughts of going out to the local for a drink or of watching an evening's TV keep on coming into my mind.'

This man's trouble is not that he suffers, as he thinks, from a weak will. His trouble is that his imagination, which is stronger than his will, is being used wrongly. It is being used to oppose his efforts to concentrate instead of to assist them. How imagination may be used for the latter purpose will be explained later on in this chapter.

What we can do about it

What, then, can be done to combat these four causes of poor concentration? First, let me briefly remind you what the causes are. They are:

1. Outer distractions.
2. Inner distractions.
3. Loss of interest in the subject-matter.
4. A conflict between imagination and will.

Here are some practical hints on removing each of these obstacles and so paving the way directly for improved concentration and indirectly for greater speed in reading.

1. *How to remove outer distractions.* To overcome this type of obstacle to concentration you must ensure that as far as possible the room where you are working is free from extraneous and unwanted stimuli.

Sit where you cannot see the traffic and pedestrians passing in the street or road or a flashing sign on a building opposite your house. Make sure that you can see properly what you are reading by sitting in good light and by having any eye defects corrected.

Shut the window so as to exclude the noise of dogs barking or radios blaring. Quietness is indispensable for concentration. Do not try to work and watch a TV programme at the same time.

Do your reading where smells from other parts of the house

will not reach your nostrils. Don't disturb your concentration by eating, drinking or smoking while you read.

Minimize the effect of stimuli of touch by sticking to one chair, table, pen or pencil to which you are accustomed.

Don't wear uncomfortable, ill-fitting clothes or shoes which constrict the feet. Read in a room where the temperature is right for you. Fresh air is an advantage but it should not be too cold. By the same token avoid a stuffy atmosphere. A temperature that gives comfortable working conditions is round about 15°C or 60°F.

If you are in pain defer your reading until the pain has been relieved. Do not try to concentrate when you have toothache or some other physical complaint that distracts attention.

See that you are seated in a comfortable posture. A desk and chair or bench should be of the right height for physical comfort and ease. Don't use a wobbly chair which will upset your sense of balance. Satisfy your eating and drinking requirements and give attention to the call of nature before you embark upon a piece of reading.

In these ways we should, when we are learning to concentrate, make things easy for ourselves by having the physical conditions that assist concentration. When material is read in isolation from other sources of stimulation it is read faster. Furthermore, if it is something we want to learn, learning is much more effective when we provide ourselves with conditions free from distraction.

2. *How to remove inner distractions.* These, we recall, are chiefly of two kinds: day-dreams and emotional conflicts.

The remedy for excessive day-dreaming is to arrange one's life so as to achieve greater satisfaction in reality. Day-dreams are a means whereby we compensate ourselves in fantasy for frustrations experienced in the real world. Any active steps taken to reduce our sources of frustration will have a favourable effect on the reduction of day-dreaming.

For example, the young man mentioned above who was addicted to day-dreaming about his sweetheart was advised to try to use his relationship with her as an incentive to studying and qualifying for a position which would enable him to marry her.

We should also try to deal with the emotional problems that distract our attention. Postman and Bruner point out that under the stress of emotional conflict we 'take in' less adequately what we read, we don't distinguish sense from nonsense so well, and we are more willing to accept unproven statements.

It is emotional conflict which interferes with concentration more than anything else. The law of attention is that one cannot attend to two things at once. While you are attending to your worries you cannot concentrate upon your reading.

To improve one's concentration, then, it is necessary to attend either to the matter in hand or else to one's worries with a view to eliminating them. But we should not expect to be able to attend to both at once.

For example, a young man was the eldest son of a family where the parents frequently quarrelled. During the first year of his career at the university he found himself unable to concentrate on his studies.

At home, when a quarrel had arisen between his parents, he sided with his mother, who was a person of mediocre educational attainments. His father, on the other hand, was a university-trained man. When he himself got to university this put him under the necessity to identify himself with his intellectually-minded father, whom he disliked. The conflict thus created proved sufficient to impair his concentration.

As a result of consulting a psychiatrist, however, he gained insight into the nature of the above conflict, and this made it possible for him eventually to 'pull himself together' and proceed with his studies.

It may not be essential to go to a psychiatrist. We may be able to do something for ourselves at home. For example, a man said: Putting into practice every day your painstaking advice on my broken love has started working in me like magic. I am a different man now. My only regret is that I did not consult you before.'

This statement was made by a man who fell in love with a girl, and was looking forward to marriage until she became pregnant by another man. This led to a break-up of their relationship and left him 'badly affected by her insincerity'.

Not the least effect was that he had been unable to give his mind to anything he took up to read – not even a newspaper.

'I am emotionally perturbed,' he had said at that time. 'I can't concentrate on anything. My mind keeps on recalling unhappy memories.'

In advising him on his problem I pointed out that his task was not to forget, but to remember without being upset by the memory. I advised him that he could do this by deliberately recalling his unhappy affair, going over and over it in his mind, familiarizing himself with the emotions it evoked, in fact, getting so used to it that it no longer disturbed him.

'This is a better way,' I concluded, 'of dealing with the problem than that of mentally "turning your back" on the memory of your broken love affair.'

3. *How to strengthen your interest in the subject-matter*. Loss of interest in the subject-matter is the third cause of impaired concentration, and this can be overcome by strengthening our interest in what we are trying to read.

To anyone who complains 'I cannot concentrate' the answer is: 'You can, if you will find something that interests you.' One of the most difficult things in the world is to try to concentrate on something that is devoid of interest for us.

As a young clerk put it: 'My concentration is poor; I would like an excellent memory – but I am bored by study.'

R.W. Emerson says: 'We remember what we understand, and we understand best what we like; for this doubles our power of attention, and makes it our own.' In other words, unless interest is present, concentration becomes extremely difficult or even impossible without an effort of will.

How can interest be developed or strengthened? Here are three suggestions that you can apply.

The first is to try to see some meaning in the subject by relating it to other subjects that do interest you or to topical events or to your daily life, or by discussing it with someone who knows more about it than you do.

For example, if you are not interested in Latin think of the language as the parent of modern languages, such as French, Spanish, Italian, etc. Try to trace connections between a Latin word like *panis* and the modern foreign words which are derived from it, e.g., *le pain, il pane, el pan,* etc.

If you want to strengthen your interest in history you might look for parallels or contrasts between people and events in, say, the Middle Ages and what is happening in the world today. Consider, for instance, the general attitude towards heresy in the Middle Ages and the wars that were fought because of it with the efforts of the churches in the world today to find a common ground of belief on which they can meet.

To see the relevance of, say, maths to the work that an intending engineer plans to do will help him to put greater effort into his studies of mathematical subjects. If he talks to someone who is already experienced in this profession the older person may be able to point out to him the usefulness of what he is trying to learn.

Secondly, use your imagination. Interest can be developed by imagining what you stand to gain by mastering the subject or what you stand to lose by not mastering it.

Suppose you are training for the teaching profession. You are required to study the history of education in this country. You find it rather dull. Remind yourself that a pass in it is essential for your teaching certificate and with it you will qualify for the kind of position you desire in the type of school you want to work in.

Thirdly, you can use auto-suggestion to strengthen your interest. You can repeat to yourself a simple affirmation such as 'This subject interests me more and more' or 'I'm learning to like this subject better every day.'

Interest alone, however, will not ensure a person being able to concentrate, as we may note from the following report of a sales representative: 'I don't seem as though I can concentrate, no matter how hard I try. It's not because I am not interested. I am indeed full of enthusiasm about the work.'

This explains why the reader should not rely wholly on developing his interest as a means of overcoming the problem of lack of concentration. Attention should also be given to the three other principles which are laid down here for tackling this problem. The last of these is the question of overcoming the law of reversed effort, to which we now turn.

4. *The law of reversed effort.* We learned above that impaired concentration can be caused by a conflict between will and imagination. The law of reversed effort states that in such a conflict imagination proves the stronger. If we try to study by an effort of will while our imagination is picturing the pleasure of doing something else our effort to study will tend to be defeated. That is why we have stressed above the value of a positive and constructive use of the imagination in developing interest.

Imagination can also be used to overcome the operation of the law of reversed effort. The law is not invoked when will and imagination work in harmony with each other.

When we will ourselves to attend, we can imagine ourselves doing so. To create a mental picture of ourselves working hard and consistently at our reading, and then to use our will-power to make the mental picture a reality is one way of solving this problem.

SELF-TESTING QUIZ

Put a tick opposite the statements which you have read in Chapter 2.

1. Understanding what you read depends on the attention you pay to it.
2. The tendency to escape from reality is to be encouraged.
3. Whether or not you listen to another person doesn't really matter.
4. Concentration makes for greater accuracy.
5. The five traditional senses are the only ones we possess.
6. Emotions interfere with our ability to study.
7. The law of reversed effort states that in a conflict between will and imagination the latter proves the stronger.
8. Quietness is inessential for concentration.
9. The law of attention states that one cannot attend to two things at once.
10. There is only one way of changing the habit of slow reading.
11. It is the easiest thing in the world to concentrate on something that is devoid of interest for us.
12. You can see meaning in a subject by relating it to other subjects that interest you.
13. You can use auto-suggestion to strengthen your interest.

✓ 14. Imagination cannot be used to overcome the operation of the law of reversed effort.

— 15. There is such a thing as trying too hard to concentrate.

Now check your answers against the answer key which you will find on page 159.

CHAPTER THREE

HOW TO READ FASTER
BY NOT TRYING

It has often been said that the human being is a creature of habit. This popular saying calls attention to an important truth which has a bearing upon our problem of reading faster. For whether we read fast or slow reading is a habit with us, like cleaning our teeth or going to the cinema.

This illustrates the role which the formation of habits plays in the individual's development. Growing up from babyhood to adulthood is largely a matter of forming useful and desirable habits and eliminating useless and undesirable ones.

The Roman orator Cicero remarks in a stoic vein, 'Great is the force of habit; it teaches us to bear labour and to scorn injury and pain.' Needless to say, this is not the only purpose which it serves. We may rightly conclude, in fact, that habit is a valuable aid to successful adaptation to the demands of life. An old saying which has much psychological truth in it runs: 'Sow an act and you reap a habit. Sow a habit and you reap a character. Sow a character and you reap a destiny.'

Habits – good and bad
A good habit is one that assists an individual's adjustment to his environment; a bad habit is one that impedes it. A habit is good if it furthers our health and well-being, physical or mental; it is bad if it injures our health or interferes with our development.

Sooner or later all of us are faced with some habit which we wish to overcome. Even if it is not a habit of our own, we may wish to help somebody else to break it. Children are apt to develop habits which distress their parents. A relative or friend may be puzzled and worried by some persistent mannerism; while, if we happen to be a professional psychologist, our main concern will be with helping and advising people who want to change their habits.

It is not surprising, therefore, that psychologists have given a good deal of attention to this problem. Their studies have made it possible to draw up certain general rules for the making and breaking of habits. It is not our intention to describe all of these, but merely to present in this chapter one of them which, on account of its effectiveness, ought to be better known than it is and is particularly adapted to the problem of improving the speed of our reading.

It is a well-known fact that attempting to overcome a bad habit by an effort of will may make it worse. For example, Mr K.N. said: 'At the age of seven I developed a habit of blinking. I tried hard to stop it but the harder I tried the worse it got.'

This is due to the operation of the law of reversed effort, which is invoked by attempting to oppose imagination with will. For example, I shall revert for a moment to the question of concentration, which I considered in Chapter 2. When you let your mind wander your imagination is given free rein. The attempt to concentrate, however, calls for an effort of will. This brings imagination and will into conflict and invokes the above law. Imagination proves the stronger with the result that the more you will yourself to concentrate the worse your mind-wandering becomes.

As long as habits remain automatic, they are carried out without a great deal of trouble. For example, once we have got into the habit of dressing or undressing in a particular way, we are able to perform these habits without any great difficulty and without paying any great attention to them. Thus our mental energies are conserved for tasks which are more difficult and require more attention.

But suppose we start consciously to attend to a habit that up to now we have carried out automatically. What happens then? Don't we find that it gives us more trouble, that the habit is more difficult to perform?

I am reminded of the story of the old man who was asked by

his grandson: 'Grandpa, do you sleep with your long beard over or under the bedclothes?' Although he had slept soundly for seventy-five years, that night the old man could not sleep. He was too busy trying to remember how he did sleep. When he attended consciously to an automatic habit, the habit was broken.

Again, suppose, for example, we are asked to give a specimen of our signature for some special purpose. We are told that we must be careful how we form the individual letters. It is a common experience to find that, in such circumstances, the ease with which we normally sign our name disappears. The task becomes as laborious as if we were doing it for the first time.

This reminds me of another story of the centipede who was asked how he managed to walk with so many legs. When he attempted to show how he did it, he got quite confused and ended up by being unable to walk at all. With him, as with us, the habit of walking had become automatic; he carried it out without paying attention to it. When he began to pay attention to it, he found that the habit was broken.

Conscious attention
This is the psychological basis of the method of negative practice or conscious attention. This method of deliberately practising a habit which you want to get rid of is psychologically sound. Professor Knight Dunlap discovered the value of it by applying it to a habit of his own. He found that he had got into the habit of repeatedly typing *hte* instead of *the*. He eliminated the habit by deliberately practising the typing of *hte*, paying conscious attention all the time to what he was doing.

The attention of other psychologists was attracted to the method. Two of them carried out an experiment in which they, too, applied it to the habit of making spelling errors. The subjects for their experiment were typing students who were just learning to transcribe from shorthand notes. Eleven students who had regularly mis-spelt four words were asked to practise retyping two of the words in their mis-spelt form and the other two words in their correct form.

Later on, when they were given a spelling test, the superiority of the method we have described was clearly shown. Ten out of the eleven students still made errors in spelling the words which they had practised correctly. On the other hand, no errors at all were made in spelling the words which had been practised *incorrectly* with careful attention being paid to the incorrect spelling.

Three other psychologists tried a similar experiment, also using words which had been mis-spelt in spelling tests. They found that the 'conscious attention' method of actually practising the habit they wished to eliminate was just as effective as the more usual method of repeating the correct spellings of the words.

An excellent illustration of the application of this principle occurs in D.H. Lawrence's novel *Women in Love*. One of the characters says: 'A very great doctor taught me ... that to cure oneself of a bad habit, one should *force* oneself to do it, when one would not do it; – make oneself do it – and then the habit would disappear.'

The novel continues:

'How do you mean?' said Gerald.

'If you bite your nails, for example. Then, when you don't want to bite your nails, bite them, make yourself bite them. And you would find the habit was broken.'

Does it work?

At this point any reader who may happen to bite his nails is probably asking himself: 'But does it work outside the pages of fiction?' The proof of the pudding is in the eating. One month after receiving the advice to try this method for nail biting a musician reported:

'For over two weeks I have not bitten my nails. This is a result of your advice. When I tell you that I have suffered from this complaint for over twenty years, you will, I am sure, realize how grateful I am.'

Other habits such as lack of concentration – and slow reading – can also be brought under control by the same method. They, too, can be got rid of by deliberately practising them, observing ourselves as we do it.

Later in this chapter we shall see how the method can be applied to improving our speed of reading. For the moment, however, let us note the reports of some students who applied it with success to the habit of mind-wandering.

For instance, a young man said: 'The theory of practising the repetition of an undesirable habit for the purpose of breaking it has helped me considerably in overcoming my lack of concentration. My memory seems to be improving too.'

Thirteen months after receiving the foregoing advice a student reported: 'I can concentrate better now.' Before receiving it he had complained: 'I find it very difficult to concentrate very long on anything. When I read a book my eyes jump upwards two or three lines, and I find myself quite often reading the same lines twice.'

Another student reported four weeks after commencing the application of the above method: 'I am finding that this cure for lack of concentration works.'

How to apply the method
How then is the method applied to improving the speed of one's reading?

Remember the basic principle: practise deliberately the habit you want to overcome. In this case it is slow reading. So this is the habit to practise deliberately.

Set aside a period of five minutes twice a day for this deliberate practice. Sit down with some reading material in hand. While you are about it you might as well read something worthwhile. I make the suggestion because it will enable you to 'kill two birds with one stone', as it were – to improve the quality as well as the speed of your reading.

Having chosen your material, deliberately read it for five minutes as slowly as you can. If you catch yourself proceeding at a normal reading pace deliberately bring yourself back to the slower rate. Force yourself by an effort of will to read more slowly than you usually do.

At the same time tell yourself that you are doing it for the purpose of stopping the habit. Imagine yourself developing a reading speed which is even better than your present one. In this conflict between will and imagination the latter will prove the stronger. The result will be that when you read anything outside your daily five-minute practice periods you will actually find yourself reading faster than you normally do.

This will be because mentally you have rebelled against imposing on yourself a limitation or restriction which you know that you can overcome.

A 49-year-old housewife to whom this method was recommended said: 'I gave this remedy of Professor Knight Dunlap's a couple of trials. It is a most degrading experience, and underlines even more strongly the conflict of wanting to do a thing one disapproves of. The idea of submitting oneself to such degradation over a prolonged period is very repulsive to me.'

Professor Knight Dunlap's method is, however, intended to be 'degrading', as this person puts it. By deliberately carrying out an undesirable habit, one is submitting to a kind of self-punishment. The idea is that you will put a stop to something that you find to be self-punishing. In other words, the method works by making use of a psychological principle known as the law of effect. This law states that an action tends to be discontinued if it proves to be unrewarding.

Like the centipede attend closely to what you are doing as you do it. Tell yourself that you are doing it with the object of breaking the habit.

I have received numerous testimonies to the value of this method. They illustrate not only its effectiveness but also its wide range of application. There are a large number of habits, both physical and mental, to which it has been successfully applied.

For example, other physical habits for which it has been used are: compulsive facial habits, such as frowning, a compulsive need to pay frequent visits to the toilet (in the absence of any organic bladder defect), sex habits, nausea and vomiting at the thought of hospitals and operations, weeping spells, biting the lips, etc.

It can also be applied to stammering, nervous and muscular tension, mannerisms, tics (involuntary muscular movements), etc.

Mental and emotional habits can also be brought under

control by the same method. They, too, can be got rid of by deliberately practising them with close scrutiny. Some habits that have proved amenable to treatment in this way are: worry, fears, lack of ease in company, being 'tongue-tied', shyness, nervousness, mind-wandering, obsessive thoughts, mistakes made while learning a skill, spelling errors, daydreaming, and so on.

It should by now be apparent to any reader how he can apply the method to his problem. All that you have to do is to bear in mind the general principle. This is: Deliberately practise the habit you want to overcome, paying careful attention to what hitherto you have done automatically.

It would be a mistake to think that the method can be applied to all habits. There are some to which it may be inexpedient to try to apply it. For example, on account of the toxic effect of repeated doses we would not recommend that it be applied to addiction to alcohol or drugs. It would also probably be impracticable to expect to use it in a case of bed-wetting.

'To bite your nails when you have a hankering for it,' writes Professor R.S. Woodworth, 'and to bite them in cold blood are really very different performances in their motivation and in their outcome. If the check-up can be so managed as to deprive a habit of its fascination, certainly a long step has been taken towards breaking the habit.'

In this passage instead of 'bite your nails' substitute 'read slowly'. The passage is then equally true of the habit under discussion in this book. Thus another famous psychologist pays his tribute to the effectiveness of the method in bringing under the control of the will something that hitherto has been carried on in spite of it.

How does it work?

Mr R.Y. offered the following comments on the technique described above:

'I read with interest about your new way to break unwanted habits. I discovered this method, too, and it works.

'But there is another side to this matter. For instance, sometimes I slip into the habit of reading well below the speed of which I know that I am capable. Instead of becoming more conscious of this habit and practising it deliberately I speed up my reading and try to take more interest in what I am studying. Then I not only feel keener but my faster rate of reading persists. This is very gratifying but I find it contradictory to your method of doing consciously what one does not want to do.

'Sometimes I can get results by practising the habit I want to develop. And yet at other times I succeed equally well by deliberately practising the undesirable habit.

'This is very puzzling to me. How do you explain it? Why doesn't consciously carrying out bad habits intensify the bad habit rather than overcome it?'

This person's comments illustrate the fact that there is more than one way of changing the habit of slow reading. The method described in this chapter and the one he has used are different approaches to the same problem. Why both should work when they seem to be opposite to each other is a problem that psychologists have not yet solved, although we may hope that they will do so eventually when more is known about habits and their formation.

You are really in the fortunate position of having two methods at your disposal for changing the habit of slow reading. The more orthodox method of 'positive practice', as it might be called, will be taken up elsewhere in this book. To realize that you have more than one weapon in your armament should be a help towards overcoming any sense of puzzlement you may share with the above person.

At first sight the method of repeating a habit deliberately does seem to conflict, as he points out, with the principle that the more you repeat a habit the stronger it becomes. The more you read slowly the slower you might expect to read. But it does not work out this way. This is because the mere repetition of any habit does not in itself make it stronger. To achieve this effect there must also be the intention to reinforce the habit. In the method described in this chapter there is no intention to do this. Consequently carrying it out deliberately does not intensify it.

This is confirmed by the reports that follow.

'I am continuing the method as per your instructions,' said a bank official. 'The deliberate practice is no trouble. The habit of slow reading is not recurring as often as it used to. I am finding, in fact, that my pace is quickening.'

A schoolmaster reported ten days after commencing the method of conscious attention: 'I have improved much generally. I have repeatedly tried the method and believe it has been of great assistance in helping me to get through the piles of books containing homework exercises which I have to mark.'

The method is really based on the principle that an action is weakened if it proves annoying. Deliberately practising a bad habit is a form of annoyance that leads to the habit being weakened.

SELF-TESTING QUIZ

Put a tick opposite the statements which you have read in Chapter 3.

1. Habit is a valuable aid to successful adaptation to the demands of life.
2. Attempting to overcome a bad habit by an effort of will is usually successful.
3. As long as our habits remain automatic, they are carried out without a great deal of trouble.
4. Slow reading can be got rid of by deliberately practising it.
5. You should force yourself by an effort of will to read faster than you usually do.
6. By deliberately carrying out an undesirable habit, one is submitting to a kind of self-gratification.
7. The law of effect states that an action tends to be discontinued if it proves to be unrewarding.
8. The number of habits to which 'conscious attention' has been applied is small.
9. It would be a mistake to think that the method can be applied to all habits.
10. There is more than one way of changing the habit of slow reading.
11. The repetition of a habit is in itself enough to make it stronger.

12. Reading matter can be classified according to the amount of scrutiny or care it demands.
13. Practice by itself makes perfect.
14. It is neither necessary nor possible that a learner should know what progress he is making.
15. The self-timing is intended to give you an idea of how much time you are spending on this book.

Now check yours answers against the answer key which you will find on page 159.

CHAPTER FOUR

YOU CAN READ FASTER IF YOU KNOW MORE WORDS

If you were to ask half a dozen people selected at random whether a palindrome is a skating-rink, a kind of spinning top or a Chinese temple, five out of six would probably reply that they didn't know. The sixth person would say that it was none of them, but merely the name given to a sentence which reads the same backwards as forwards. Admittedly five out of six people would attach no practical importance to a knowledge of the meaning of the word palindrome. Nevertheless the number of words we know and use can materially affect the ease and speed with which we read. And this, of course, can affect our success and position in the world.

The English language is a miscellaneous collection of some five hundred thousand words. A child of five knows about five hundred of these – or one-thousandth of the total. The average adult is acquainted with perhaps two per cent and uses regularly considerably fewer. The better-educated person knows about two or three thousand more. If you do not know the meaning of the word palindrome, it is ten to one that about ninety-eight per cent of your mother tongue is unexplored territory to you. Consequently, as you try to improve your speed of reading you are more than likely to meet words whose meaning you are not familiar with. Such words tend to make you stop and think. This naturally slows the pace which you are trying to build up.

So now we understand why it is important that in your efforts to read faster you should acquire a larger English vocabulary.

How words affect your earning power

But I get along all right with my two per cent, you say. But do you? Have you considered the possibility that you would get on a great deal better if you knew a few more of the words you at present do not know?

An enquiry was conducted some years ago by the Human Engineering Laboratory of Hoboken, New Jersey. It examined the relation between the range of a person's vocabulary in terms of the number of words he knows and his earning power in terms of hard cash.

The method of the enquiry was to administer tests in the use of vocabulary to thousands of business people, and it was found in practically every case that an extensive range of vocabulary coincided with the possession of a large income. One significant fact revealed by the enquiry was that a large vocabulary was not so much related to the amount of education a man had received as to his position in the business world.

There is one fact brought out clearly by a little time spent in reflection on the careers of famous men. That fact is that the ease with which we express ourselves is greater or less in proportion to the number of words we have at our command. Upon our facility in mastering the ideas set down by others and communicating our ideas to our fellow men depend the impression that we create and the success or failure of the personality or venture that we are trying to put over.

Moreover, any person who has ever done much reading at all must have felt that one of the writer's greatest difficulties is to find the *mot juste* – the exact word to express the shade of meaning that he wishes to convey. And the more successful he is in finding it the greater the writer. We intuitively recognize the skill of the author when the words he uses make his meaning crystal-clear to us. We welcome such a writer with open arms because we have to wade through so much reading the meaning of which is muddy because the writer's thoughts are unclear.

Yet gone are the days – if they ever existed – when the literary artist could be content merely to make his meaning plain – he must also make it forceful, compelling, interesting.

Besides their serving the useful end of communication we expect the words we read to carry beauty, strength and the ability to draw the attention and sway the opinions of the reader.

Of course, it is manifestly impossible for anyone to learn all the rich variety of words that is at his disposal, much less use it. Not only would he have insufficient time in the span of a single life, but he would never be able to keep pace with the growth of the language. The virility of a language, like that of a child, is measured by its growth; and the English language has such a phenomenal capacity for growth that it has borrowed words from almost every other language in use on the face of the earth. A third factor that we should bear in mind is that much of our vocabulary consists of technical and scientific words known only to specialists in particular branches of knowledge.

But we need to keep pace to some extent. We have only to observe how our language has grown in the last year or two to appreciate the necessity of keeping abreast of the linguistic times. A few years ago no one had heard of words like astronaut, Chunnel, supermarket. To-day so wide is their currency that they and many others equally as new are on everybody's lips. If we are to be successful with our reading and in our business and social lives it is essential that we should keep track of the introduction of new words and let our vocabulary grow as the language itself grows.

Abuse of language

It was a cynic who said that the purpose of language is to disguise meaning rather than to reveal it. But when one reads reports of those in authority answering questions put to them in Parliament, there appears to be some justification for this view. However much we may deplore the situation, one half of the world's troubles is due to people who use words to propagate lies, and the other half to those who use them to conceal the truth.

Therefore the necessity is all the more forcibly brought home to the ordinary man and woman of recognising a spade when it is called a digging implement. He or she will then be in a position to distinguish between people who carelessly misuse words because they know no better and those who wilfully misuse them when they ought to know better.

The English have often been accused of not knowing their own language. Certainly foreigners who learn English have a greater command of the language than many Englishmen. It is difficult to say where the responsibility for this state of affairs rests, but part of it must surely be laid at the door of our system of primary and secondary education.

A cursory examination of the school-leaver of sixteen suggests that his education has been confined to learning to write his own name illegibly, to adding two and two so as to make five, and to becoming indifferent not merely to reading faster but to reading at all.

A task on which the schools do not place sufficient emphasis is that of making to-morrow's citizen fit for struggling with the realities of life. When one considers how ill-equipped many pupils are who leave school at sixteen, one must admit that their training leaves much to be desired.

A wider knowledge of the printed word is the first thing that a person requires to enable him to co-operate intelligently with his fellow men and make a success of his life. A system of instruction which acquaints him with only about two per cent of the wealth of words in his native language cannot by any means be said to be efficient.

One of the reasons why the world is peopled with mediocrities, why so many people drift through life without reaching any heights of achievement is simply that they do not possess a tenth of the tools to do the job. Deprived of the means of influencing their fellow men, of carving out a niche in the world for themselves and of achieving success, they drift along using the same hackneyed words day after day, the same doggerel phrases, the same worn-out clichés.

What other language has a hundred and seventy-five words to describe beauty, yet how often do we fall back on 'nice'? Where else do we find the wealth of words that English uses to describe colours, yet how often do we meet in our reading the half-dozen or so names given to the colours of the spectrum?

How far would science have advanced if it had had to rely

on Anglo-Saxon to give voice to its discoveries and had been unable to draw upon the vast word-forming resources of Latin and Greek? What else has made English literature the greatest in the world but the pre-eminence of its writers and the skill with which they have handled and arranged combinations of English words?

Brush up your vocabulary

Here are six ways in which you can enlarge your vocabulary:

1. By finding and studying synonyms.
2. By finding and studying antonyms.
3. By adding prefixes to words.
4. By adding suffixes to words.
5. By forming masculine and feminine words.
6. By the use of phrasal verbs.

Let us study each of these ways in detail.

1. *You can enlarge your vocabulary by finding and studying synonyms*. A synonym is a word that is similar in meaning to a given word. Thus 'enumerate' is a synonym of 'count'. 'Weighty' is a synonym of 'heavy'. 'Individual' is a synonym of 'person', and so on.

A synonym is not always an exact equivalent in meaning of another word. For instance, are 'agreement' and 'concord' exact synonyms? No, not exactly. It is true that both mean 'mutual understanding, harmony' or 'treaty'. But agreement is usually between people, whereas concord can be between persons or things. However, there can be agreement between things in the grammatical sense, as in the sentence 'The verb agrees with its subject in number and person'. 'Concord', too, can be used in this sense. An agreement can exist in law in the sense of a binding contract between parties. This is a meaning which 'concord' does not have. 'Concord', on the other hand, can occur in music, i.e., a chord which is satisfactory in itself without others to follow. 'Agreement' cannot be used in this sense.

Let us take a verb and study the synonyms which we can

find for it. Consider the verb 'walk'. Here are some synonyms:

clump, hike, march, mince, pace, perambulate, plod, promenade, prowl, ramble, roam, rove, saunter, shuffle, slouch, stagger, stalk, stray, stride, stroll, strut, stump, tiptoe, toddle, totter, traipse, tramp, trudge, wander.

Although all these verbs are expressive of the same physical action, each makes some slight addition to the meaning of the basic verb 'walk'. This can be seen more clearly by setting out their meanings as follows:

clump – walk heavily
hike – walk vigorously
march – walk with regular paces
mince – walk with affectedly short steps
pace – walk with slow regular steps
perambulate – walk up and down
plod – walk doggedly
promenade – walk up and down in a public place
prowl – walk furtively
ramble – walk without a definite route
roam – walk at random
rove – walk without fixed destination
saunter – walk leisurely
shuffle – walk dragging one's feet
slouch – walk in an ungainly manner
stagger – walk unsteadily
stalk – walk slowly with long steps
stray – walk aimlessly
stride – walk with long steps
stroll – walk leisurely
strut – walk pompously
stump – walk as with a wooden leg
tiptoe – walk on the points of the toes
toddle – walk with short unsteady steps
totter – walk feebly
traipse – walk wearily
tramp – walk with firm heavy tread
trudge – walk slowly and painfully
wander – walk without a settled plan

The above list illustrates how, starting from a basic verb, we can enlarge our vocabulary by finding synonyms which add something to its meaning. We should try the same process with other words, referring to the dictionary or to a reference work for the synonyms we want and their meanings.

2. *You can enlarge your vocabulary by finding and studying antonyms*. An antonym is a word opposite in meaning to a given word. For example, 'high' is an antonym of 'low', 'insert' is an antonym of 'extract', and 'heat' is an antonym of 'cold'.

Let me select a few words and try to find suitable antonyms for them. I choose these words at random, and in some cases the meaning of the word may not permit an antonym. But you should not assume this until you have racked your brains in an effort to find the right one. This exercise will prove invaluable for enlarging your vocabulary.

Here, then, is a list of words picked at random from the commonest words in the English language:

everything	hurry	often	taste
gain	just	send	tomorrow
heaven	matter	space	wind

everything. What is the antonym of 'everything'? This is an easy one. Few people will fail to give the correct answer 'nothing'.

gain. 'Lose' is the first word that comes to mind. This is the antonym of 'gain' in its more usual meanings. A less usual meaning of the word is 'reach, arrive at', as in the sentence 'The ship gained the harbour.' What is the antonym of 'gain' in this sense? 'Miss' suggests itself as the right word.

heaven. Antonym: 'hell'.

hurry. This word is both a noun and a verb. As a noun its antonym is 'slowness' or 'sloth'. As antonyms to the verb we might choose 'lag', 'tarry', 'slacken', or 'delay'.

just. It is difficult to imagine an antonym to 'just' when used as an adverb, as in the sentence 'Just tell me what to do.' But in the sense of 'fair' we have 'unfair' and 'undeserved' as antonyms. 'Unjust' and 'improper', too, may have occurred to you.

matter. Here we have 'spirit', 'mind', 'form', 'manner', according to the sense in which we use this word as a noun. If we use it as a verb, there is the following antonym: 'be unimportant'.

often. Antonyms: 'infrequently', 'rarely', 'uncommonly', etc.

send. This common verb has a variety of meanings with a consequent variety of words of opposite meaning. 'Bring', 'withhold', 'retain', 'keep', 'fail to move' are some possible antonyms of this verb.

space. Antonyms: 'close up', 'cramp', 'confinement', 'matter'.

taste. 'Distaste', 'tastelessness', 'feast', 'lack of taste', 'insipidness' provide antonyms of different meanings of this word.

tomorrow. 'Today', 'the past' or 'yesterday' come to mind.

wind. 'Calm', 'run down', 'strings', 'breathlessness', 'unwind' and 'go straight' are all possibilities here. Each is an antonym of 'wind' in a different meaning of this word as noun or verb.

An exercise of this kind, simple as it appears, is nevertheless one that calls for some ingenuity. It certainly helps to make one familiar with a larger range of words. And the more words we succeed in getting to know the more power we give ourselves to read faster. We thus overcome one of the principal obstacles to faster reading – having to pause to wonder what this or that word means in a particular context.

3. *You can enlarge your vocabulary by adding prefixes to words*. A prefix is one or more syllables added at the beginning of a word to qualify its meaning.

Here is a list of common prefixes:

a-, ab-, ad-, amphi-, an-, ana-, ante-, anti-, arch-, auto-, be-, bi-, cata-, circum-, co-, contra-, counter-, de-, dis-, dys-, en-, (em-), epi-, ex-, extra-, for-, fore-, hemi-, hyper-, hypo-, in-, inter-, intro-, meta-, mis-, mono-, non-, out-, over-, pan-, para-, per-, peri-, post-, pre-, pro-, re-, retro-, semi-, sub-, super-, syn-, trans-, ultra-, un-, under-, up-, with-.

Some of these are of Latin or French origin, some are of Greek origin, while some are of purely English origin. All of them can be used to enlarge one's vocabulary by putting them in front of words.

For example, take the common prefix 'un-' and see how many words it can combine with. Thus we have: unable, unafraid, un-American, unbecoming, unbeliever, unbroken, unbuilt, uncertain, unchain, unchanging, unclean, unclear, and so on.

Or consider how many new words can be formed by the addition of the prefix 'over-'. Some examples are: overdo, overdone, overdraw, overdress, overdrive, overdry, overdue, overeat, overfill, overfull, overgrow, overhang, etc.

'Trans-' is capable of being prefixed to a large number of words, such as transact, transfigure, transform, transplant, transposition, trans-ship.

Here are some examples with 'for-': forbear, forgive, forbid; and with 'fore-': foremost, foresee, foretaste, foretell, foreword.

Here is a list of negatives in 'in-' and its variant 'im-':

Negatives in 'in-'

    action – inaction
    complete – incomplete
    dependent – independent
    direct – indirect
    experience – inexperience
    famous – infamous (pronounced *in*famous)
    human – inhuman

Negatives in 'im-'
The following words form their negative in 'im-':

    balance – imbalance
    possible – impossible
    probably – improbably
    polite – impolite

'Un-' and 'in-' are perhaps the commonest prefixes used for forming antonyms, but another common one is 'dis-'. Here is a list of words in which this prefix is used:

disable	disarm	disfavour	disown
disagree	disbelieve	dishonour	displease
disallow	discontinue	dismount	distrust
disappear	discount	disorder	disuse

4. *You can enlarge your vocabulary by adding suffixes to words.* A suffix is a syllable or syllables added at the end of a word to qualify its meaning.

Here is a list of common suffixes:

-able, -age, -ance, -ant, -ary, -craft, -dom, -ed, -en, ence, -ent, -er, -ery, -ess, -fast, -fold, -ful, -hood, -ible, -ing, -ious, -ise (-ize), -ish, -kin, -less, -let, -like, -ling, -ly, -ment, -ness, -or, -ory, -ous, -ship, -some, -stead, -ster, -uous, -ward(s), -wise, -wright, -y.

Here are some words which illustrate the use of suffixes:

able – ably
accept – acceptable, acceptance
according – accordingly
account – accountable, accountant
act – actor
admit – admissible, admittance
age – aged, ageless, ageing
agree – agreeable, agreement
allow – allowable, allowance
bag – bagful, baggy
burn – burner, burning
busy – busily
cup – cupful
cut – cutter, cutting
dream – dreamer, dreaming, dreamless, dreamlike, dreamy
dry – drily, dryer, dryness
favour – favourable, favoured
fit – fitful, fitting, fitment, fitness
form – formless
full – fuller, fullness, fully, fulsome
glass – glassful, glassy
hand – handful, handsome, handy
honour – honorary, honourable

Prefixes and suffixes together are known as 'affixes'. According to Dr Rudolph Flesch, the number of affixes in any given 100 words of reading material has an important bearing upon the ease or difficulty – and so the speed – with which it can be read. Dr Flesch says that if there are less than 54 the material qualifies as not very difficult. If there are 54 or more the material can be regarded as very difficult.

This means that whether we are training ourselves to improve our speed of reading of difficult or less difficult material, we shall get along better if we familiarize ourselves with the affixes which are to be found in it.

5. *You can enlarge your vocabulary by acquainting yourself with masculine and feminine forms of words.* Many English nouns have two forms according to whether they are applied to men or women, or to male or female animals. Here are some examples which you should note.

actor – actress	hart – roe
alto – contralto	hero – heroine
bachelor – spinster	host – hostess
barman – barmaid	lad – lass
baronet – dame	landlord – landlady
boar – sow	marquis – marchioness
buck – doe	masseur – masseuse
bullock – heifer	monk – nun
cob – pen	patriarch – matriarch
cock – hen	peacock – peahen
colt – filly	proprietor – proprietress
comedian – comedienne	ram – ewe
czar – czarina	sire – dam
dog – bitch	stag – hind
duke – duchess	stallion – mare
earl – countess	sultan – sultana
emperor – empress	testator – testatrix
executor – executrix	tragedian – tragedienne
fox – vixen	traitor – traitress
gander – goose	usher – usherette
god – goddess	widower – widow

6. *You can enlarge your vocabulary by the use of phrasal verbs.* A phrasal verb is a verb combined with an adverb or preposition,

e.g., 'go *up*', 'go *on*', etc. For example, although the verb 'to get' is often overworked, it is one of the most useful words in the English language, and is especially useful when it forms part of a phrasal verb.

The following sentences illustrate how it is thus used:

'You will never get away with it' (succeed in doing it).
'The rider got down from his horse' (dismounted).
'He got off lightly' (escaped).

Similarly, one can *get about*. This means 'go from place to place'. It also means 'begin walking after illness', e.g., 'After being in bed so long, he is now getting about again'. It can also refer to rumours, e.g., 'How did that story get about?'

A successful candidate in an election is said to *get in*. The harvest is also got in; one gets in, too, when one boards a train. To get one's hand in means to become familiar with some skilled job. There is a common saying that 'one can't get a word in edgeways (*or* edgewise).' This is used when someone is monopolizing the conversation.

Someone who becomes friendly with a person of the opposite sex is said to get off with that person. Someone who is approaching a certain age is getting on for sixty, seventy, etc. A situation that one cannot control gets out of hand.

The phrasal verb 'to get up' is particularly useful on account of its variety of meanings, some of which are illustrated by the following examples:

'At what time did you get up?' (rise from bed).
'The wind is getting up' (beginning to be violent).
'Let's get up a dance' (organize it).
'That certainly got my back up' (made me angry).
'That is nicely got up' (arranged).
'I am getting up this subject for an examination' (working at it).

'To acquire a large and usable vocabulary,' counsel Dwight E. Watkins and Herbert F. de Bower, 'is by no means an easy task. It requires close attention to words over a long period of time ... The best way to enlarge one's use of words is to build them into one's life. This may be done by entering into life

fully with a high spirit of curiosity – by studying everything
that comes under one's attention, by learning the words that
are connected with it ... He should be able to spell the words
and to pronounce them correctly.'

Improving pronunciation

In order to improve your pronunciation, you should take note
of the way that educated people pronounce their words. You
should do your best to imitate the pronunciation that they
adopt without, of course, making yourself too conspicuous in
your speech. It is better to mispronounce a word and appear
natural than to pronounce it correctly and appear forced.

When in the course of your reading you come across a word
that is new to you, take the trouble to look it up in a good
dictionary. Note not only the meaning but also the
pronunciation. You will need to refer to the key to
pronunciation that you will find in the introductory pages of
the dictionary. After you have learned the pronunciation in
this way, try to make opportunities for using the word in
speech.

It is always helpful in learning a new word to examine
carefully how you heard or saw it used. When you think you
understand it, use it in a sentence of your own. Try it in
conversation or in a letter. Make it a part of your vocabulary.
Until you have used a new word, it doesn't really belong to
you.

When you describe something, use the words that are
necessary to make your statements definite. Try to say exactly
what it was, how it looked, what effect it had on you. Words
added to your vocabulary in this way increase the clarity and
force of your speaking and writing as well as the speed of your
reading.

If you are an average teenager your vocabulary should
consist of about 9,000 words. An average adult should know
about 11,700 words, while a superior adult will know about
13,500 words.

If you seek further help in improving your vocabulary you
can obtain it by consulting the well-known *Hartrampf's
Vocabulary-Builder*. This provides synonyms, antonyms and

words of related meaning.

The value of an improved vocabulary is a means not only of reading faster but also of improving self-expression and increasing efficiency generally.

Word-knowledge tests

Appended below is a set of word-knowledge tests on which the person who wishes to read faster may try his strength. The first and last few letters are given in each case to provide a clue to the word. All you need to do is to supply the rest of the word. The number of dots corresponds with the number of missing letters. Check the extent of your vocabulary by scoring two points for each correct word. If you come to grief over the spelling of a word, count one point. When you have finished the tests turn to pages 63-64, where the correct answers are given.

If you score 100 points or more you may congratulate yourself – you are very favourably placed to improve your reading speed; indeed, in all likelihood you are already a successful man or woman in your own sphere. Scores between 75 and 100 are satisfactory, although it cannot be denied that there is room for some improvement. If your score is below 75 points you have done well, but there is room for a good deal of improvement.

LITERATURE

1. A collection of words that makes sense   S E . . . . C E
2. A figure of speech in which a comparison is made   S I . . L E
3. The author of *Robinson Crusoe*   D E . . E
4. A metrical foot containing two syllables   I A . . I C
5. Picture-writing   H I . . . . C S
6. An outline or summary of a book   S Y . . . . I S
7. The publisher's recommendations which appear on a book jacket   B . . . B

8. The oldest epic in the English
   language   BE...LF
9. A short poem expressing the
   writer's sentiments   L...C
10. A manuscript containing two
    sets of writing   PA......ST

SCIENCE

1. One who strove to transmute
   base metals into gold   AL.....ST
2. A minute particle of matter   MO....LE
3. A theory put forward by
   Einstein   RE......TY
4. One of the planets   JU...ER
5. A device for measuring changes
   of temperature   TH......ER
6. A method by which heat is
   transmitted   RA....ION
7. The branch of knowledge which
   deals with antiquities   AR......GY
8. The discoverer of radium   C..IE
9. The positive part of an atom   PR...N
10. The outer ring of the earth's
    atmosphere   ST.......RE

RELIGION

1. A person who is not a Jew   GE...LE
2. A name given to Christ
   meaning 'the Anointed One'   ME...AH
3. A system of teaching by the
   method of question and answer   CA.....SM
4. A statement of religious belief   C...D
5. A set of rules regarding
   religious conduct   CA..N
6. The ten commandments   DE.....UE
7. Certain scriptural writings the
   authenticity of which is in doubt   AP.....HA

8. The last book of the New Testament   R E . . . . . I O N
9. The belief in a personal God   T . . . S M
10. A Mohammedan priest   M U . . . I N

PSYCHOLOGY

1. Past experiences retained in the mind   M E . . R Y
2. A famous Russian physiologist   P A . . O V
3. An innate impulse   I N . . . . C T
4. An automatic response to a stimulus   R E . . . X
5. The ability to perceive relationships between things   I N . . . . C E
6. A predominant state of feeling   S E . . . . . N T
7. A psychological disorder   N E . . . . I S
8. An American school of psychology   B E . . . . S M
9. A splitting of the personality   S C . . . . I A
10. The damming up of a strong desire   R E . . . . . I O N

MUSIC

1. An extemporised composition   I M . . . . I O N
2. A piece of music played at a funeral   R E . . . E M
3. A person of wide musical experience   M A . . . R O
4. A musical term signifying decreasing in volume   D I . . . . . . D O
5. An interruption of the regular musical beat   S Y . . . . . . I O N
6. A musical instrument of Hawaiian origin   U K . . . L E
7. The predecessor of the piano   H A . . . . . . R D
8. The entire range of an organ   D I . . . . O N

9. A musical composition for full
   orchestra   S Y . . . . N Y
10. Two or more notes played
    together   C H . . D

GENERAL KNOWLEDGE

1. A person who hates his fellow
   men   M I . . . . S T
2. The conclusion of a speech   P E . . . . . I O N
3. A universal remedy   P A . . . E A
4. Putting off till to-morrow what
   can be done to-day   P R . . . . I O N
5. An adjective meaning 'worldly'   M U . . . N E
6. A chronological record of
   seasons, etc.   A L . . . A C
7. One who has reached his
   eightieth year   O C . . . . A N
8. A time when day and night are
   of equal length   E Q . . . O X
9. A place for the temporary
   disposal of bodies   M O . . . . R Y
10. To make a detailed list   I T . . . S E
11. The entrance to the underworld
    in classical mythology   A V . . . U S
12. An officer next above a captain   M . . . R
13. A self-evident truth   T R . . S M
14. Disbelief   S C . . . . . . S M
15. A Greek philosopher   P L . . O

ANSWERS TO WORD-KNOWLEDGE TESTS
(See pages 60-63)

Literature: (1) Sentence; (2) Simile; (3) Defoe; (4) Iambic; (5)
Hieroglyphics; (6) Synopsis; (7) Blurb; (8) Beowulf; (9) Lyric; (10)
Palimpsest.

Science: (1) Alchemist; (2) Molecule; (3) Relativity; (4) Jupiter;
(5) Thermometer; (6) Radiation; (7) Archaeology; (8) Curie; (9)
Proton; (10) Stratosphere.

Religion: (1) Gentile; (2) Messiah; (3) Catechism; (4) Creed; (5) Canon; (6) Decalogue; (7) Apocrypha; (8) Revelation; (9) Theism; (10) Muezzin.

Psychology: (1) Memory; (2) Pavlov; (3) Instinct; (4) Reflex; (5) Intelligence; (6) Sentiment; (7) Neurosis; (8) Behaviourism; (9) Schizophrenia; (10) Repression.

Music: (1) Improvisation; (2) Requiem; (3) Maestro; (4) Diminuendo; (5) Syncopation; (6) Ukulele; (7) Harpsichord; (8) Diapason; (9) Symphony; (10) Chord.

General Knowledge: (1) Misanthropist; (2) Peroration; (3) Panacea; (4) Procrastination; (5) Mundane; (6) Almanac; (7) Octogenarian; (8) Equinox; (9) Mortuary;)10) Itemise; (11) Avernus; (12) Major; (13) Truism; (14) Scepticism; (15) Plato.

SELF-TESTING QUIZ

Put a tick opposite the statements which you have read in Chapter 4.

1. The number of words we know and use can materially affect the ease and speed with which we read.
2. One of the writer's least difficulties is to find the *mot juste*.
3. It is possible for anyone to learn all the rich variety of words at his disposal.
4. The English have often been accused of not knowing their own language.
5. 'Enumerate' is a synonym of 'count'.
6. 'Insert' is an antonym of 'extract'.
7. A prefix is added at the end of a word to qualify its meaning.
8. You can enlarge your vocabulary by adding suffixes to words.
9. The number of affixes in any given 100 words of reading material has an important bearing on the speed with which it can be read.
10. You can enlarge your vocabulary by acquainting yourself with masculine and feminine forms.
11. A phrasal verb is a verb combined with an adverb or preposition.
12. It is better to pronounce a word correctly and appear natural than to mispronounce it and appear forced.
13. Until you have used a new word, it doesn't really belong to you.
14. When you describe something, use the words that are necessary to make your statements indefinite.
15. An average adult should know about 11,700 words.

Now check your answers against the answer key which you will find on page 159.

CHAPTER FIVE

THE LINE AND CARD TECHNIQUES

The first task in this chapter will be to measure your normal reading speed. An idea of what speed you normally read at will provide a useful comparison with what you can achieve after training.

For this purpose read the following passage. You will need a watch to time yourself. Read at your normal rate without any conscious effort to speed up.

Start reading and timing yourself *now*:

In the heart of rural England is born ...

AN EXPERIMENT IN EDUCATION

'Most people think reading, writing and arithmetic are dull and monotonous, but I find them interesting.' These words were written by 13-year-old Pauline Jackson, who attends the village school of Offord Cluny and Offord Darcy. She and her fellow senior scholars have carried out an experiment in education under the guidance of Mr J.W. Crick, the village schoolmaster.

The Offords are modestly described by Lt-Col O.N.D. Sismey, the squire's son, as 'only a typical English village.' The two parishes lie approximately half-way between Huntingdon and St. Neots. The main road through the village, the River Great Ouse and the railway line from King's Cross are all within one hundred yards of each other.

A village existed in this part of rural Cambridgeshire before the Conqueror's men compiled the Domesday Book. In spite of their long history, however, education in the Offords is as up to date as the 80-mile-an-hour expresses that thunder through what was once Offord Station.

One day during a school discussion Mr Crick's pupils suggested: 'Why not write a book about our village?' 'Optimistic voices proclaimed the idea,' records the head master, 'and thus book and title were born.' The inhabitants of Offord are justly proud of *Two Parishes – One Village* (W. Goggs & Son Ltd., 116 High Street, Huntingdon), which their children have produced.

A happy set of people live in Offord, the children tell us. There is Mr W. Storey, who, says Lionel Boyce, aged 14, 'is such a happy man that everyone who knows him calls him "Happy Bill".' The shopkeepers have a cheery word for their customers. 'When we open the door,' writes 12-year-old Gina Simpson, 'Mrs Dudley comes into the shop and happily serves us.' In Offord Cluny Mrs Hurst, says Ellen Wayman, aged 11, 'opens at nine in the morning and closes at ten at night. She always seems happy and I think she is a very good shopkeeper.'

Of course, the rough goes with the smooth in the Offords. When Dennis Colbert, aged 12, asked Mr J. Dudley, the roadman, whether he liked cleaning drains, he replied: 'Not much.' Dennis himself, however, likes his job. On Saturdays and in the holidays he helps Mr Croot, who 'cycles round Offord, starting about half past eight, with about two hundred newspapers and magazines and twenty comics.'

Another Offordian who is happy in his work is Mr J. Leaden, who appropriately enough is the plumber. After interviewing him, Gina Simpson reported: 'He told me that plumbing is hard, but after several years he still finds it very interesting.'

When Jacqueline Simpson, aged 11, interviewed Mr Hawkins, the carpenter, he not only told her all about his trade but he also shared with her his philosophy of life: 'Put all you can into life; you will then be able to get something out of it.'

Local studies, history, geography, architecture, rural science, folk-lore, have come to have meaning and interest to the children, because they have found out things for themselves. Sound psychology provides the basis of the experiment. In the words of Mr Crick the idea behind it is: 'When children attend school because they like attending the resulting benefits are immeasurable. The best means of achieving this end is to make the school work alive and interesting.'

How the head master's philosophy works out in practice may be judged from the words with which we began this article. He is preparing his pupils to take their rightful places in the world by helping them to develop pride in and responsibilities for the community in which they live. Education, in his view, 'is the training and forming of the mind and character as well as the absorption of knowledge.'

'The school,' he adds, 'still tries to give the children of Offord every educational advantage within its power.' *Two Parishes – One Village* is evidence that shows how well it is succeeding. What the children of Offord have achieved will long be talked about in the houses and farms that lie along the banks of the Great Ouse in the heart of rural England.

Now stop reading and timing yourself. Write your time in minutes and seconds in the box below:

minutes	seconds
4	2 6

Multiply the minutes by 60 and add on the seconds. Write your time in seconds here:

seconds
2 6 5

The length of the passage is 700 words. Therefore divide 700 by your time in seconds. Multiply the answer by 60. This number is your normal reading speed in words per minute.

Write the number in the box below:

My normal reading speed is now [1 5 8] *words per minute.*

You will probably find that this number is somewhere around 200. If so your reading speed is average. If it is rather less than this you are a slower reader than average. But take heart. With practice you can improve your standard to average or beyond. If your reading speed is rather higher than 200 you can congratulate yourself, for you read faster than average already. Thus you have a good start towards greatly increasing your speed.

When you get to the end of the book you will be able to look back and compare the new reading speed you have attained with the figure you have written above. This should serve to give you an encouraging indication of the progress you have made through submitting yourself to the training and practice which this book affords.

Did you pay attention to *comprehension* in reading the above passage? You want to be able to understand what you have read. To test how well you mastered the thought of this passage take the following comprehension test. Answer the questions by putting a tick against (*a*), (*b*) or (*c*) according to which you think is correct.

COMPREHENSION TEST
An Experiment In Education

1. Who finds the three R's interesting?
   (*a*   Pauline Jackson.
   (*b*)   Gina Simpson.
   (*c*)   Dennis Colbert.
2. Where are Offord Cluny and Offord Darcy?
   (*a*)   In Bedfordshire.
   (*b*)   In Cambridgeshire.
   (*c*)   In Hertfordshire.
3. Has Offord a railway station?
   (*a*)   Yes.
   (*b*)   No.
   (*c*)   We aren't told.
4. The title of the children's book is:
   (*a*)   *One Village – Two Parishes.*
   (*b*)   *Two Villages – One Parish.*
   (*c*)   *Two Parishes – One Village.*

5. Who wrote about Mrs Hurst?
    (a) Lionel Boyce.
    (b) Ellen Wayman.
    (c) Jacqueline Simpson.
6. What is Mr Croot?
    (a) A carpenter.
    (b) A plumber.
 — (c) A newsagent.
7. Who interviewed Mr Leaden?
    (a) Gina Simpson.
    (b) Dennis Colbert.
    (c) Lionel Boyce.
8. What is Mr Hawkins' philosophy of life?
    (a) 'Look after yourself, for no one else will.'
    (b) 'Get something from life by putting your best into it.'
 — (c) 'Keep your eyes open and your mouth shut.'
9. What is the village schoolmaster's name?
 —(a) Mr Crick.
    (b) Mr Storey.
    (c) Mr Dudley.
10. He thinks that education should:
    (a) Concentrate on absorbing knowledge.
    (b) Encourage children to work on Saturdays.
 — (c) Make school work alive and interesting.
Turn to page 82 for the correct answers to these questions.

The line technique

Now, having got the question of your normal reading speed out of the way, let us turn to our subject proper. I propose to give you two principles of rapid reading, to illustrate them in action, and to give you practice in using them.

The first one is as follows:

1. *Aim at taking in a line at a time.*

The first practical technique is based on the fact that ordinarily we read one word at a time. The eyes start at the left of the line of print and travel across the page, pausing, taking in a word, moving on, pausing again, taking in another word, and so on. This process is naturally slow; indeed it is needlessly slow, because the human eye is capable of taking in more than one word at a time.

The first aim, then, is to give up the habit of reading a word at a time. You want to replace it with the habit of reading a phrase, a sentence, a whole line, even two lines at a time.

To do this, abandon the practice of starting at the left of the line and working across the page. Instead fix your attention on the *centre* of the line. No longer work *across* the page; work *down* the centre of the page from line to line.

Move your eyes slightly about the axis of the centre of the line, trying to take in the whole line in two or three glances. Then move on to the next line and treat that in the same way. Your gaze moves *down* the page from line to line instead of from left to right across one line and then back to the beginning of the next line.

'Learn to take in more words at each glance,' counsels Norman Lewis. 'The word-by-word reader unnecessarily slows himself up by as much as 50 per cent. If your concentration and comprehension are good, you can easily train yourself to read *phrases* instead of *words* – and thereby make a significant increase in speed.'

The card technique
2. *Cut out that looking back.*

The second technique to which I wish to introduce you is that of eliminating the bad habit of looking back at words which you have already read. If you observed yourself as you read the test passage for measuring your normal speed, you may have noted that you indulged in this practice. You glanced back at words a line or two above the line you were supposed to be reading.

This jumping to and fro of the eyes from one line to another, combined with the habit of reading by words, naturally accounted for slowing down your speed of reading. Therefore, if you can cut out this habit it will make a further contribution towards increasing your speed of reading.

'Eye-movement photographs of some 12,000 readers,' writes James I. Brown in an article 'Diagnosing Your Reading Problem' (*Modern Medicine*, September 1970), 'show that college students regress an average of 15 times in reading only 100 words. To be sure, they perform better than the average sixth-former, who regresses 20 times, and are superb when compared with the average primary school pupil, who regresses 52 times in reading 100 words. Regressive eye movements may take up, therefore, an estimated one-fifth to one-half of the usual reading time, depending upon their frequency. This makes them a major limiting factor on reading speed.'

That is why I want you to try the exercise that follows. Draw a line in pencil down the centre of the pages on which the following passage appears. Then take a postcard or a piece of stiffish cardboard of the same width as the pages of this book. Hold the card in both hands and as your eyes follow the centre line slide the card down the page, cutting off the lines which you have already read.

Let me repeat: The idea is to restrain yourself from glancing back over what you have already read. Continue to push on with your reading even if details here and there are not clear to you. You will lose nothing by not reading odd words twice – which is all that your former habit amounted to. And you will gain a lot in terms of an improved reading rate.

Remember to correct this habit of 'backtracking' by sliding your card down the page, holding it in both hands and letting the eyes follow the line down the centre.

Now start reading the following passage in accordance with the above instructions. You need not time yourself.

Practice Material – I

ANCIENT LIGHT ON MODERN PROBLEMS

On a quiet street in one of America's west-coast cities lives a middle-aged Swami, or Hindu teacher, who numbers among his disciples such well-known contemporary literary figures as Christopher Isherwood and Gerald Heard. Swami Prabhavananda, as he is known, is engaged in teaching Vedanta, a philosophy based on the most ancient scriptural writings of Hinduism, which were current more than a thousand years before the birth of Christ.

Since he first went to America in 1923 he has done much to popularize Vedanta in the western world, and has translated, with Christopher Isherwood, a poem which comprises one of the best-known portions of Hindu scripture.

This poem, known in Sanskrit as Bhagavad-Gita and in English as *The Song of God*, is mainly in the form of a dialogue between Prince Arjuna, descendant of an ancient line of kings, and Sri Krishna, his charioteer, who is a personification of God. Sri Krishna explains that concentration of the will leads to absorption in God. A man's aim should always be to establish himself in the consciousness of the Atman, to cultivate the realization of his indwelling godhead.

The path that a man follows to attain enlightenment is determined by his temperament. The path of knowledge is for the contemplative: the path of action for the active. The aim of both is to achieve union with Brahman or the Universal Intelligence.

Sri Krishna then proceeds to give some instructions on the practice of yoga and the postures to be adopted for that purpose. He issues a warning that yoga is not for the man of intemperate habits in eating or fasting, sleeping or waking.

Arjuna raises the objection that if union with Brahman is to be of any value it must be permanent; and yet it demands concentration of the mind, the normal action of which is one of constant oscillation of attention. To this Sri Krishna replies that the mind can be brought under control by constant practice.

But what, continues Arjuna, happens to the man who begins the practice of yoga and then falls by the wayside when he finds it too difficult for him? Sri Krishna replies that even such a man will win the rewards of the doer of good deeds. After he dies he will be reincarnated into an illumined family, so that he can still carry on the work begun in his former life.

Arjuna then asks Sri Krishna to explain to him the nature of Brahman and of the Atman. 'Brahman is that which is immutable,' replies Sri Krishna, 'and independent of any cause but Itself. When we consider Brahman as lodged within the individual being, we call Him the Atman.' In other words, Brahman is the Universal Soul, while the Atman is the individual soul.

In response to Arjuna's request Sri Krishna vouchsafes to Arjuna a revelation of his divine nature. Arjuna acknowledges Sri Krishna's power and might and pays homage to him.

Sri Krishna explains that provision is made in the Hindu religion for all types of devotees. Those who cannot become absorbed in Brahman are recommended to reach their goal by concentration; or if they lack this power they should devote themselves to good works. If they cannot do even this, the path of self-surrender may be followed.

The most sacred truth that Hinduism teaches is that he who knows Brahman as the supreme Reality knows all that can be known. He who has realised this truth becomes truly wise. The purpose of his life is fulfilled. That wisdom is 'the secret of secrets', 'the deepest of all truths', 'the supreme truth of the Gita'.

The message of the Gita

What is the message that the teaching of *The Song of God* brings to modern man? For our present purpose it may be considered in relation to two fields: occupation and anxiety. In each of these fields *The Song of God* has something to say that is of value.

It teaches that a man should work for the work's sake only and not for the fruits of the work, maintaining evenness of temper in both success and failure. Work done with anxiety about the results is held to be inferior to work done in a spirit of devotion to the task.

One must learn what kind of work to do, what kind of work to avoid, and how to reach a calm state of detachment from one's work. One should not shrink from doing what is disagreeable to him, nor should he long to do what is agreeable.

The Song of God describes four types of workers: the seer, the leader, the provider and the server. The seer's duty is to be tranquil in mind and spirit, and to practise habits of virtue and temperance. His primary aim is to pursue wisdom and truth. The leader's duty is to cultivate courage, skill, and mercy towards his foes, and to be resolute at the head of his own people. The providers are the traders, farmers and breeders of cattle. The duty of the servers is to labour for others.

Success does not consist in a server becoming a seer, but in each following his duty, which is laid down by the laws of his nature. He who does this will attain perfection. A man's own natural duty, even if it seems imperfectly carried out, is better than well-performed work for which he is not by nature fitted.

According to *The Song of God*, all action of whatever kind is involved in imperfection; therefore, no one should give up the work for which nature has best fitted him, even if at present he is not performing it efficiently. His aim should be to improve his efficiency.

The Song of God prescribes a liberating attitude which banishes anxiety and other negative states, such as grief, anger and envy. This mental attitude is usually described as non-attachment. It might also be called indifferent assurance. Non-attachment is defined by the Gita as the abandonment of the fruits of action. A quiet mind is achieved by accepting both pleasant and unpleasant experiences with equal impartiality and indifference.

The claim is made that the assumption of this attitude of mind enables one not only to endure unpleasant circumstances with equanimity, but also to learn from them the lesson that they teach. This is that we are attracted to them because they correspond with our state of soul-unfoldment. In short, Vedanta teaches us to seek within ourselves the reason for every failure rather than to blame it upon other people or circumstances.

Claude Bragdon, in *Yoga for You*, tells a story which, he says, taught him in a practical way the advantages of non-resistance. One day when as a young boy he was sitting on his grandfather's knee, the old gentleman got hold of a handful of his hair. The lad jerked his head first one way and then the other in an effort to free himself, crying, 'Grandpa, you're hurting me! You're pulling my hair!' 'No,' replied his grandfather, 'you're pulling your own hair. If you would keep still it would not hurt at all.'

The Gita instructs the victim of worry to ask himself whether he is not pulling his own hair. The remedy is to stop struggling. Those who think that the teaching of the Bhagavad-Gita is as far divorced as it can be from Christianity should reflect that Christ also taught: 'Resist not evil.'

An attitude of non-attachment or indifferent assurance enables one to participate in life's manifold experiences without suffering the disillusion which comes inevitably with the realization of their transient nature.

Now take the following comprehension test.

COMPREHENSION TEST
Ancient Light On Modern Problems

1. Vedanta is:
   (a) A cult practised in cellar clubs on the Left Bank in Paris.
   (b) A philosophy based on the scriptural writings of Hinduism.
   (c) A style of women's clothes worn in Outer Mongolia.
2. *The Song of God* is:
   (a) The title of a play by William Shakespeare.
   (b) The name of one of the books of the Old Testament.
   (c) A dialogue between Prince Arjuna and Sri Krishna.
3. The state of union with Brahman or the Universal Intelligence is called:
   (a) Enlightenment.
   (b) Disillusionment.
   (c) Apartheid.
4. Is yoga for the man of intemperate habits?
   (a) Yes.
   (b) No.
   (c) The author doesn't say.
5. What happens to the man who finds yoga too hard for him? Sri Krishna's answer to this question is that:
   (a) He will continue his good works in another life.
   (b) His conscience will plague him with feelings of guilt.
   (c) He should try something else.
6. 'That which is immutable.' This is Sri Krishna's description of:
   (a) Non-attachment.
   (b) Brahman.
   (c) The reward of work.
7. Work done in a spirit of devotion to the task is:
   (a) Superior to work done for the sake of the reward.
   (b) Inferior to work done for the sake of the reward.
   (c) Neither better nor worse than work done for the sake of the reward.

8. Courage, mercy and resolution are attributes of:
   (a) The seer.
   (b) The leader.
   (c) The server.
9. *The Song of God* says that the worker should:
   (a) Strive to become another kind of worker.
   (b) Give up the work for which nature has fitted him.
   (c) Seek to improve his efficiency.
10. Non-attachment is:
    (a) The abandonment of the fruits of action.
    (b) The withdrawal from participation in life.
    (c) The revolt against experiences of failure.

Turn to page 82 for the correct answers to these questions.

Practice Material – II

You have now learned two major techniques for improving your reading speed. One is to look at the centre of the page and read downwards instead of across. The other is to avoid looking back at words which you have already read.

Now you can combine these two techniques by reading the following passage as you practise both. Draw your centre lines as before. Use your card too. But note the time as you start and when you stop. Read as rapidly as you can. But don't make a deliberate effort of will. Rather use your imagination. Imagine yourself reading faster than usual. But in the main let the techniques which we are teaching you effect their own improvement in your reading speed. As you continue to practise them you can rely on their doing this automatically without your making any special effort to read faster.

Of course, as you get used to these new habits you can dispense with the artificial aids. You can imagine your line drawn down the centre instead of actually drawing it. And you will get so used to pushing on down the page without looking back that you will be able to do without the use of the card. For the time being, however, you should continue to use these aids until you find yourself able to read faster even without them.

Now, having drawn your lines and with your card at the ready, time yourself on the following passage.

Start timing yourself and reading *now*:

THE MYSTERY OF SHAKESPEARE'S LOVE LIFE

It is a strange paradox that of the life of the greatest figure in English literature we should possess but the barest details. If we were to say that William Shakespeare was born in 1564 at Stratford-on-Avon, that he married Anne Hathaway, had three children, went to London, made his name as a playwright and actor, retired to Stratford, bought a house, died and was buried, this is about all that we can glean from historical documents and church registers.

Fortunately, for information about the mind of the poet we have the evidence of the plays themselves, assuming, of course, that they were written by William Shakespeare, although even this is disputed in some quarters.

If we read the plays in their chronological order, it is possible to trace in them the development of the poet's mind. They fall naturally into three stages corresponding roughly to the periods of youth, maturity and retirement.

As R.W. Emerson puts it, 'Shakespeare is the only biographer of Shakespeare.'

Comic Period

The first period is the period of comedy and includes such works as *A Midsummer Night's Dream,* which is pure fantasy, showing Shakespeare's youthful genius at its best; the historical comedy *Henry IV*, in which appears Falstaff, Shakespeare's greatest comic figure; *Much Ado About Nothing*, which is a comedy of wit; *As You Like It,* a pastoral comedy; and *Twelfth Night*, a comedy of intrigue.

When Shakespeare left home for London he carried with him from his native Warwickshire fields an enduring love of nature. While this is a feature of all his work, it is seen at its best in these early plays. *A Midsummer Night's Dream* provides a good illustration of this quality. The atmosphere of the play is redolent of

'A bank whereon the wild thyme blows,
Where oxlips and the nodding violet grows.'

The general tenor of the plays of this period is the peace and harmony exemplified by natural beauty.

The three plays *Much Ado About Nothing, As You Like It,* and *Twelfth Night* are commonly held to mark the height of Shakespeare's comic genius; and from high comedy there is a sudden transition to high tragedy.

Tragic Period

The first great tragedy of Shakespeare's second period is *Julius Caesar.* The tragic note is sustained through *Hamlet* and *Othello,* until we touch the depths in *King Lear* and *Macbeth.* Afterwards the gloom is lightened somewhat with *Antony and Cleopatra.*

It would be idle to pretend that so sudden and marked a transition did not correspond with some equally profound change in the mentality of the poet himself; and a clue to the nature of this change is hinted at in the Sonnets, which are undoubtedly autobiographical. Two themes run prominently through the Sonnets. One is the inconstancy of a dark lady with whom the poet was infatuated. The other is mingled reproaches and affection for a young man.

The facts seem to be that Shakespeare was in love with a woman and that he lost her to a friend to whom he was also deeply attached. The young man has been identified as Henry Wriothesley, Earl of Southampton, to whom the Sonnets are dedicated, but the identity of the woman is an unsolved mystery. She is generally referred to as the Dark Lady of the Sonnets.

The dynamic cause of the tragic period may have been the betrayal of the poet by Southampton. Like Antonio in *The Merchant of Venice,* Shakespeare, too, appears to have lost a friend through a woman. The theme of a friend's ingratitude is prominent in the plays of this period.

Even in *Much Ado About Nothing* Claudio had concluded that

'Friendship is constant in all other things
Save in the office and affairs of love.'

Again, in *As You Like It* we note:

'Blow, blow, thou winter wind,
Thou art not so unkind
As man's ingratitude.'

And now in *Julius Caesar* we find that the crux of the play is Brutus' ingratitude towards and betrayal of his friend Caesar. We also observe King Lear's complaints of the ingratitude of his daughters. We see Macbeth behaving treacherously towards his host and king, while in *Timon of Athens* the hero is the victim of the ingratitude of friends, and Coriolanus suffers the ingratitude of the Roman populace.

One feels that into the character of Hamlet Shakespeare has put much of what he himself must have felt at this period of his life. Hamlet has been robbed of his mother by his uncle just as Shakespeare had been robbed of his mistress by his friend. Hamlet's jealousy of his uncle, who has married his widowed mother, gives an outlet to the poet's feelings that he, too, had been supplanted in the affections of another. As Freud says, 'It can, of course, be only the poet's own psychology with which we are confronted in Hamlet.'

The theme of ingratitude in *King Lear* is accompanied by powerful feelings of disgust with sex. The reader is left in no doubt that Shakespeare himself was disgusted with sex and that his attitude towards women was one of contempt. Having suffered at the hands of a particular woman, he takes a poor view of women in general. This tendency to confuse the part with the whole is an unconscious mental mechanism which might be called generalization.

A favourite motif in the tragedies is that of the good man brought to ruin by a bad woman. For example, Macbeth is led into murder by the ambitions of his wife. The old King Lear is driven out into the storm by his daughter Goneril.

Finale

The Shakespeare who wrote the tragedies is a different man from the earlier Shakespeare of the comic period, and different again from the Shakespeare of the period of retirement. In this latter period we find evidence of calm after the storm. It is significant indeed that one of the plays of this period is *The*

Tempest. A note of reconciliation is struck, of acceptance of life's trials and conflicts – as though the poet had learned the lessons of experience and had come to regard with pity and tolerance the frailties of mankind.

The wheel thus completes full circle as it does in every life. The mystery is no longer a mystery. We find that the lack of documentary evidence about Shakespeare's career is not an obstacle to the understanding of his love life. In the Sonnets and in the plays themselves we can trace the story for which no other evidence is available. It is as though in writing the plays the poet had been writing his autobiography.

That great creative works are autobiographical is true in a wider sense too. Not only does the writer reveal himself in his writings, but the artist bares his soul in a painting and the conflicts of the musician are externalized in his scores. Each in his individual way acts as his own best biographer and to regard creative productions from this point of view can only serve to heighten our enjoyment of them and to intensify our realization of the extent to which the artist truly expresses himself in his works.

Now finish reading and timing yourself.
Note your time in this box:

minutes	seconds

Convert your time into seconds by multiplying the minutes by 60 and adding on the seconds. Write the answer here:

seconds

The length of the above passage is 1,200 words. Divide 1,200 by your time in seconds and then multiply the answer by 60. This gives you your reading speed for this passage in words per minute. Write it here:

My reading speed is now [   ] *words per minute.*

Compare what you have written above with what you have written on page 67. You may be pleasantly surprised to notice that your reading speed has increased already.

'How can I learn to read quickly without having to pronounce the words mentally?' asked Mrs A.R. 'It's not that I actually pronounce them. I only imagine doing it. I have a vivid imagination, so can easily do that.'

This is the first question which this chapter has attempted to answer. Its answer has been that an adult should be capable of grasping the thought of a passage by sweeping his eyes down the page without the need of the child's habit of whispering the words. You can give yourself practice in sweeping your eyes down the page by drawing lightly a pencil line down the centre. Keep your gaze fixed on this pencil line, reading down the page from line to line instead of across each line from left to right.

In addition you need to give yourself further practice in cutting out looking back as you read. For this you have been recommended to use the card technique described on page 69-70.

Continue practising these two techniques to consolidate the habits which you have begun to acquire in this chapter.

SELF-TESTING QUIZ

Put a tick opposite the statements which you have read in Chapter 5.

1. Our first task in this chapter will be to measure your normal reading speed.
2. This provides a useful comparison with what you can achieve after training.
3. If your reading speed is around 200 words per minute you are a faster reader than average.
4. The first technique is to aim at reading one word at a time.
5. Instead of working down the page we should work across each line.
6. 'There is no point in training yourself to read phrases,' says Norman Lewis.
7. We need to prove to ourselves that our understanding has not been affected.
8. The second technique is to cut out that looking back.

9. Jumping to and fro from one line to another slows down your speed of reading.
10. You will lose a great deal by not reading odd words twice.
11. You can combine these two techniques.
12. Will yourself to read faster than usual.
13. You can imagine your line drawn down the centre instead of actually drawing it.
14. You cannot do without the use of the card.
15. You can rely on the techniques without making any special effort to read faster.

Now check your answers against the answer key which you will find on page 159.

ANSWER KEYS TO COMPREHENSION TESTS
An Experiment In Education
(*See* page 69)
1. (*a*); 2. (*b*); 3. (*b*); 4. (*c*); 5. (*b*); 6. (*c.*); 7. (*a*); 8. (*b*); 9. (*a*); 10. (*c*).

Ancient Light On Modern Problems
(*See* page 75)
1. (*b*); 2. (*c*); 3. (*a*); 4. (*b*); 5. (*a*); 6. (*b*); 7. (*a*); 8. (*b*); 9. (*c*); 10. (*a*).

Multiply your total of correct answers in each comprehension test by 10. This gives your score as a percentage and you can keep a record of it by entering it on the chart provided on page 160.

CHAPTER SIX

THE PENCIL AND TWO-LINE TECHNIQUES

A common fault of slow readers is that they tend to make unnecessary movements. They follow the words with their finger. They move the head from side to side. They mouth the words, whispering them to themselves as they read. Even if this movement of the lips is suppressed they may say the words mentally to themselves.

The Pencil Technique

1. *Eliminate bad habits such as whispering and pointing.* A child learning to read forms the words with his lips and may even say them aloud and follow the print with his finger. An adult should be capable of grasping the thought of the passage merely by sweeping his eyes down the page without the need of the child's habits of whispering and pointing.

I have already given you practice in sweeping your eyes down the page without pointing. You have done this by drawing your pencil line down the centre of each page. I want you to continue to do this, or if you feel that you can trust yourself to keep to the centre of the page, you can omit the drawing of the pencil line.

Similarly I want you to continue to avoid the habit of glancing back at words which you have already read. I have tried to discourage this by giving you the exercise with the piece of cardboard. Whenever you feel that you have cured yourself of the habit of looking back you can dispense with the use of the cardboard.

For the moment, however, should you wish to continue with

the pencil lines and the cardboard, please feel free to do so. In addition I want to give you a further exercise for cutting out unnecessary movements of the lips while reading. For this you will need to use your pencil again.

So, if you want to, draw your pencil lines and use your cardboard while reading the following passage. In addition hold the pencil between your teeth in order to avoid lip movements.

Are you ready? Right! Then read the following passage in the manner prescribed above.

Practice Material – III

THE MAN WHO DISTURBED THE SLEEP OF THE WORLD

Sigmund Freud, the founder of the modern psychology of the Unconscious Mind, was born on 6th May, 1856, in Freiberg, a small town which at that time was in Austria but is now in Czecho-Slovakia. His mother, Amalie, was the young second wife of Jakob Freud, a Jewish wool merchant whose business had for some time been steadily declining.

The decline in trade led to the Freud family giving up their home in Freiberg and moving, when Sigmund was three, first to Leipzig and then to Vienna, which at that time was still 'gay Vienna'. Here in the Jewish quarter Sigmund and his younger brother and five younger sisters grew up and received their education. For eight years Sigmund attended the Sperl Gymnasium or High School, which, after distinguishing himself by his prodigious memory and passion for book-learning, he left to become a medical student at the University of Vienna.

His decision to take up medicine was influenced by his hearing Goethe's essay on Nature read aloud at a popular lecture. 'In my youth,' he afterwards wrote, 'I felt an overpowering need to understand something of the riddles of the world in which we live and perhaps even to contribute something to their solution.'

At the University, which he entered in 1873, Freud studied physiology under the famous teacher of his day, Ernst Brücke, in whose laboratory he worked until 1882. On taking his degree as Doctor of Medicine in 1881, he became engaged to his future wife, Martha Bernays.

Pressed by the need to earn money and support himself, he left the physiological laboratory and entered the General Hospital in Vienna as an assistant. Soon afterwards becoming a junior resident physician, he was attracted to the study of brain anatomy under the renowned psychiatrist, Meynert.

In 1885 he was appointed Lecturer in Neuropathology at the Hospital on the strength of a number of papers he had published on organic diseases of the nervous system. In the same year he was awarded a travelling grant which enabled him to visit Paris to study the work of the famous French psychiatrist, Charcot.

At the Salpêtrière, the Parisian insane asylum, Charcot demonstrated the phenomena of hypnotism, which he considered to be a manifestation of hysteria. On his return to Vienna in 1886, Freud married and set up in practice as a specialist in nervous diseases, using the method of hypnotic suggestion that he had learned from Charcot.

Because he felt his own hypnotic technique to be inadequate, Freud returned to France in 1889 to study at Nancy the work of Liébeault and Bernheim, who believed that the phenomena of hypnotism were due to suggestion. From both Charcot and the Nancy School Freud derived hints that encouraged him to formulate his views about the existence of unconscious mental processes and about the origin of neurosis in sexual maladjustment.

Later on Freud became dissatisfied with the method of hypnotic suggestion and also with the method of catharsis devised by his colleague Breuer, with whom he collaborated in publishing *Studies on Hysteria*. Freud then developed the method of 'free association', in which the patient is invited to say whatever comes into his or her mind, regardless of whether it is considered unimportant, irrelevant or shameful.

The results achieved by free association led to the discovery of the concept of 'repression', by which the patient refuses to become aware of painful memories and emotions.

In 1900 Freud published *The Interpretation of Dreams*, which puts forward the view that the dream is capable of being understood with the help of free association. The book is generally considered to be Freud's masterpiece. 'Insight such as this,' he himself wrote of it, 'falls to one's lot but once in a lifetime.'

It was in *The Interpretation of Dreams* that Freud mentioned for the first time the Oedipus complex – the male child's rivalry with his father for the affections of his mother. He described it in the following words: 'King Oedipus, who slew his father Laius and married his mother Jocasta, merely shows us the fulfilment of our own childhood wishes.'

This monumental work was followed by *The Psychopathology of Everyday Life*, in which he put forward the view that errors, like dreams, have their roots in the Unconscious Mind.

As might be expected, opposition developed to Freud's views, especially to his theory that the sexual function starts at the beginning of life. With the publication of *The Interpretation of Dreams* he was accused of 'disturbing the sleep of the world'. The spirit of independence with which Freud met this opposition carried him through until he began to gather round him a small circle of supporters. These disciples included Adler and Jung, who were later to break away from him and found their own schools.

Meanwhile Freud had been given the title of Professor Extraordinary at the University, and was delivering regular lectures to small audiences of psycho-analytical converts. In 1909 he went to America, where he gave five lectures on psycho-analysis at Clark University, Worcester, Massachusetts.

In 1907 and 1910 Freud published two books in which he analysed the relation between the Unconscious and artistic creation. They were *Delusion and Dreams in Jensen's 'Gradiva'* and *Leonardo da Vinci: A Psycho-Sexual Study of an Infantile Reminiscence*.

He then turned his attention to religion and in 1912 appeared the first of his investigations of that topic, *Totem and Taboo*, in which he attempted to explain religion in terms of the Oedipus complex. Towards the end of his career he wrote *Moses and Monotheism*, a further contribution to the study of the psychology of religion.

In 1923 Freud underwent the first of several operations for the cancer of the jaw that had begun to afflict him and that was eventually to kill him. Nevertheless his literary output continued undiminished. In 1925 appeared *An Autobiographical Study*, which is more an account of his theories than of his life. To this period, too, belong *The Future of an Illusion, Civilization and its Discontents, Beyond the Pleasure Principle* and *The Ego and the Id*.

The first two are investigations of the origins of religion and morality. *The Future of an Illusion* is an attack upon religion, which it stigmatizes as a flight from reality. *Civilization and its Discontents* traces the course of man's search for happiness in a culture which demands the renunciation of instinctual pleasure. In *Beyond the Pleasure Principle* Freud postulated a duality of life and death instincts, and in *The Ego and the Id* he outlined the division of man's mind into the ego, which is partly conscious and partly unconscious, the id, which is wholly unconscious, and conscience or the super-ego.

On the rise of the Nazi regime in Germany Freud's books were burned there in 1933. Even when the Nazis marched into Austria, Freud was reluctant to leave the country. But one day in 1938 he returned to his house at 19, Berggasse, Vienna, to find the Gestapo there. His passport and money were confiscated, he was forbidden to continue his work, and the entire stock of books belonging to his publishing house was destroyed.

On hearing this news, Dr Ernest Jones, the leading psycho-analyst in this country, flew to Vienna to try to persuade Freud to leave. Eventually he was successful but not before the Nazis had demanded a heavy ransom. Princess George of Greece, who had been psycho-analysed by Freud, offered the Nazis the quarter of a million Austrian schillings she had on deposit in a Vienna bank. It was not until President Roosevelt had interceded, however, that the Nazis finally agreed to accept this sum and let Freud go.

Freud left Vienna for the last time on 4th June, 1938, travelling on the Orient Express to Paris and thence to London, where Dr Ernest Jones had found a house for him in Hampstead. It was here that he resumed his work, completing the final draft of *Moses and Monotheism* and also starting to write his last work, *An Outline of Psycho-Analysis*.

This work was interrupted by his death, which occurred on 23rd September, 1939. He was cremated at Golders Green, where his ashes are preserved in a vase mounted on a marble column bearing the simple inscription, 'Sigmund Freud 1856-1939'.

In appearance Freud was, to quote one of his disciples, 'slender and of medium size. He had deep-set and piercing eyes and a finely shaped forehead, remarkably high at the temples.' He wore a short dark-brown beard and was a chain-smoker of cigars.

Freud had six children, three boys and three girls. Of his descendants two deserve special mention. His daughter Anna has carried on her father's psycho-analytical work. His grandson Lucien has distinguished himself as a painter.

It is impossible to assess adequately in a few words Freud's impact upon Western civilization. 'An overpowering need to come at the truth at all costs,' writes Dr Ernest Jones in his biography of Freud, 'was probably the deepest and strongest motive force in Freud's personality.' The world is indebted to him for his greatest contribution to the truth – his discovery of the Unconscious Mind. It was he who explored for the first time this vast hinterland of mental life, and laid bare the deeper knowledge that we possess to-day of the truth about human nature.

Now, as before, test yourself on your understanding of the thought content of the above passage. Answer the following questions by putting a tick against what you think is the right answer.

COMPREHENSION TEST
The Man Who Disturbed the Sleep of the World

1. 'The man who disturbed the sleep of the world' was:
    (a) Leonardo da Vinci.
    (b) Ernest Jones.
    (c) Sigmund Freud.

2. Where was Freud educated?
   (a) Vienna.   (b) Leipzig.   (c) Hampstead.
3. What influenced him to take up medicine as a career?
   (a) Visiting Charcot at the Salpêtrière in Paris.
   (b) Hearing Goethe's essay on Nature read at a lecture.
   (c) Having his money and passport confiscated by the Gestapo.
4. Freud was married to:
   (a) Princess George of Greece.
   (b) Anna Freud.
   (c) Martha Bernays.
5. Who believed that the phenomena of hypnotism were due to suggestion?
   (a) Liébeault and Bernheim.
   (b) Adler and Jung.
   (c) Brücke and Meynert.
6. 'Repression' means:
   (a) Refusing to become aware of painful emotions.
   (b) Saying aloud whatever comes into one's head.
   (c) Understanding dreams with the aid of free association.
7. The Oedipus complex is:
   (a) The male child's rivalry with his father for the love of his mother.
   (b) The view that errors have their roots in the Unconscious Mind.
   (c) The theory that the sexual function starts at the beginning of life.
8. *The Future of an Illusion* is:
   (a) An explanation of religion in terms of the Oedipus complex.
   (b) An attack upon religion as a flight from reality.
   (c) A study of the conflict between culture and man's quest of happiness.
9. Freud's death occurred in:
   (a) London.   (b) Paris.   (c) Vienna.
10. What was the title of Freud's last work?
   (a) *An Outline of Psycho-Analysis.*
   (b) *Beyond the Pleasure Principle.*
   (c) *An Autobiographical Study.*

Turn to page 97 for the correct answers to these questions.

The Two-line Technique

2. *Reading two lines at a time.* The second technique to which I want to introduce you in this chapter is an advance on the second one in the previous chapter. This, you will remember, involves fixing your gaze on the centre of the line and trying to take in as much of the line as you can in one or two glances.

Now I want you to try the same thing with the following passage, but this time try to take in two lines at a time. You will not find this easy, but don't worry if you don't succeed at first. Remember, the techniques are simple, but their perfection depends on how much practice you give them. I want you to know what the techniques are and then I rely on you to practise them whenever you do any reading.

So read the following passage, applying to it the techniques which you have already learned. Use the cardboard if necessary and also the pencil between your teeth. In addition draw your pencil line down the centre of the pages. This time, however, instead of fixing your gaze on the centre of each *line*, start by fixing it on the centre of the *space* between lines 1 and 2. Take in as much of the first two lines as you can. You probably won't be able to do it in one glance but try to use as few glances as you possibly can. When you have got the thought of the first two lines transfer your gaze to the centre of the space between lines 3 and 4. Take in the thought content of these lines in as few glances as you can manage. Then proceed to the centre of the space between lines 5 and 6.

If you like, before you start this exercise you can go down the pencil line you have marked and add crosses at the points where you are supposed to look. These pencilled crosses will serve as focusing points for your gaze as you work down each page trying to take in two lines at a time.

Are you clear about what you are supposed to do? There are four things which are required of you as you read the following passage. They are:

1. Draw your line down the centre of each page and mark crosses on it at the centre of the space between each pair of lines.
2. Use your cardboard to cut off the lines you have already read.
3. Hold a pencil between your teeth to stop unnecessary lip movements.

4. As you read the passage try to take in the thought content of two
lines at a time in as few glances as possible.

Remembering what you have been taught so far read the
following passage, applying the four techniques in the way
that you find suits you best. Have a wrist watch at hand to
time yourself as you read. Start to read and time yourself *now*:

Practice Material – IV

25th July, 197–

Miss P. Owens,
27 Fairfax Parade,
Blisworth,
Worcs.

CHILD GUIDANCE REPORT

The key to the understanding of the behaviour problems of
children is provided by the word 'conflict'. The so-called
'naughty' child is in conflict with his environment and his
'naughtiness' is the natural expression of that conflict. The
term 'environment' must be understood in a wide sense, and
includes more than the physical things with which the child is
surrounded; it includes also social and school influences and
in particular the emotional atmosphere in which the child has
been and is being brought up at home.

Hence your first contention is correct, that given favourable
circumstances and especially an emotionally mature home
atmosphere the average child will grow into the normal adult.
It is equally true, of course, that while the environment of the
child is in any way abnormal, the child's development will be
stunted, and the more serious the abnormality, the more harm
is done to the child. 'Give me the first five years' is a plea that
many child psychologists have echoed since it was first
uttered.

The ideal remedy for the child whose development is seen to
be diverging from the normal is to control the child's home
environment. In time this will be done by making education
for parenthood compulsory. But until that era is ushered in,
the best that the teacher can generally do is to control the
child's school environment and to some extent the social

influences to which he is exposed, i.e., his relations with other children. Indeed the teacher is frequently reluctant to interfere in family matters, knowing quite well that the average parent feels that no one can bring his own children up so well as himself.

Before I suggest the ways in which the teacher can influence the child's development by controlling his school environment, it will be useful to note that the three children, Richard, John and Helen, are at a stage of development the chief characteristics of which are:

1. The child's behaviour is largely governed by his instincts, which clamour for immediate satisfaction. But he learns gradually to inhibit those which are antisocial. The frustrations which his instinctive drives meet with build up the system of inner prohibitions called the conscience. A too lax training produces an over-indulgent conscience; a too strict one produces an over-exacting conscience.
2. The child is gradually acquiring a growing sense of physical and emotional independence, although he is never completely independent of his environment.
3. There is an exuberance of imagination. The youngster delights in fairy-tales and make-believe activities.
4. The child's tendency to achieve self-assertion by repeating the familiar is a compensation for those situations in his environment which produce feelings of inadequacy.
5. The child begins to grow out of the auto-erotic stage of sexual development, which is seen in the infant's love of its own body. Other loves (e.g., of parents, brothers, sisters, etc.) require a modification of this self-love. The behaviour of which you complain in John is a regression to an earlier technique by which the young child subconsciously draws attention to himself by displaying his body.

Practical recommendations
1. *Intelligence*
The antisocial child is frequently handicapped by subnormal intelligence as well as by an adverse environment. You do not mention the intelligence levels of the three children, but I presume that you are familiar with the two rival views of

intelligence which now hold the field, the Spearman two-factor theory and the theory of general abilities held by Terman and others. The general conclusion reached in this field is that intelligence is innate and the best that the educationalist can do is to raise the child to his innately determined potential maximum. If this happens to be below average, the educational system must accommodate itself to the child and not vice versa. This is usually carried out in practice by measuring the I.Q.s of the children and segregating the backward (as distinct from those merely retarded by emotional factors) into special classes or special schools. Some investigation along these lines would help you to determine whether your three children are really backward or merely retarded.

2. *The child must be made to feel that he matters and that he has a place to fill in the little world of the school.*

 The teacher can do much to counter the adverse effects of the home environment in this respect by:

(*a*) Giving the child little responsibilities and duties.

(*b*) By giving praise where praise is due and withholding condemnation as much as possible.

(*c*) By encouraging the child to obtain mastery over material things, i.e., manual activities. Your approach to Richard via paper aeroplanes is good. The only way in which the child can regain confidence in his own abilities is through being encouraged to use them and be successful in doing things.

3. *Redirection versus suppression.*

If John shows a fondness for taking chalk out of school it may mean that he has never owned anything that was really his, and hence has had no outlet for his acquisitive instinct. His energies for acquiring things, therefore, must not be suppressed, for this will aggravate the trouble, but rather be re-directed into socially desirable channels. For example, Dr Agatha H. Bowley in her delightful little book *The Natural Development of the Child* suggests that the school should encourage collections of silver paper, conkers, marbles, and later, picture postcards, stamps, autographs, butterflies, wild flowers, news items, newspaper photographs, and nature specimens.

4. *The importance of social contacts.*

It is a truism to say that man is a social animal and thrives on contact with his fellow men. The importance of social contacts and friendships cannot be over-estimated, and the young child whose upbringing has driven a wedge between him and other children by making him suspicious, resentful and unco-operative must be led to overcome these undesirable qualities by means of corporate activities and group play. Play activities are rightly given a prominent place in the junior school, and it is important that the child who lacks confidence or draws attention to himself in antisocial ways should be as successful in playing with other children as in learning manual skills, number, etc.

The play projects of the junior school will help these three children in other directions also. They utilise their love of 'make-believe'. They counter the tendency of the young child to invent imaginary playmates when his lack of confidence prevents him from associating with real ones. Furthermore, they assist his development by encouraging the play propensity, which is as important to the adult as to the child. And finally, play allows the child to work off the emotional intensity which has been bottled up by circumstances outside the school.

5. The success which you can report in the case of Helen is most encouraging, and there is no reason why similar treatment based upon the lines here described should not prove equally successful with the two boys. The teacher knows that in applying these methods, which are designed to help the child to recover confidence, gain a sense of security and overcome his antisocial tendencies, she will earn the gratitude of the child in later years.

Now stop reading and timing yourself. Write your time in the box below:

minutes	seconds

Convert your time into seconds. (Multiply the minutes by 60 and add on the seconds.) Write the answer here:

```
┌─────────────────┐
│   seconds       │
├─────────────────┤
│                 │
└─────────────────┘
```

The length of this passage is 1,220 words. To find your reading speed divide 1,220 by your time in seconds and multiply the answer by 60. Write the answer here:

My reading speed for the above passage is [   ] *w.p.m.*

Compare this speed with the speeds which you have achieved before on the timed passages. You should be encouraged to note the progress which you are continuing to make.

Finally, to make sure that you have understood what you have read at this new speed take the following comprehension test. The answer key will be found on page 97.

COMPREHENSION TEST
Child Guidance Report

1. What is the key to the understanding of children's behaviour problems?
   (a) To know that the problem is an expression of conflict.
   (b) To believe that sparing the rod means spoiling the child.
   (c) To realise that the child has been exposed to too much TV.
2. What does the average child's development towards maturity demand?
   (a) A reduction in the price of sweets.
   (b) A favourable environment.
   (c) A Welfare State.
3. Why is the teacher reluctant to interfere in family matters?
   (a) Because it would mean his getting the sack.
   (b) Because he isn't paid to do so.
   (c) Because he knows that parents think they are best qualified to bring up their children.
4. What are the names of the three children to whom this report refers?
   (a) David, Roger and Susan.

  (b) Richard, John and Helen.

  (c) Kenneth, James and Sandra.

 5. What do the child's instincts clamour for?

  (a) Immediate satisfaction.

  (b) Ultimate frustration.

  (c) Social adjustment.

 6. Is the child ever completely independent of his environment?

  (a) Yes.

  (b) No.

  (c) The report doesn't mention the matter.

 7. What does the child's exuberance of imagination lead to?

  (a) Disappointment.

  (b) Bullying of other children.

  (c) Delight in fairy-tales.

 8. What is the antisocial child frequently handicapped by?

  (a) Lack of brothers and sisters.

  (b) A subnormal intelligence.

  (c) Disinterested parents.

 9. Complete this sentence. Intelligence is ...

  (a) Innate.

  (b) Instinct.

  (c) Average.

10. How can a child regain confidence in his abilities?

  (a) By being encouraged to use them successfully.

  (b) By being slapped and scolded for his lack of confidence.

  (c) By being made to go to church and attend Sunday school.

Turn to page 97 for the correct answers to these questions.

SELF-TESTING QUIZ

Put a tick opposite the statements which you have read in Chapter 6.

1. A common fault in slow readers is that they tend to make unnecessary movements.

2. A child learning to read forms the words with his lips.

3. An adult should grasp the thought of the passage by sweeping his eyes down the page.

4. Continue the habit of glancing back at words which you have already read.

5. Hold the pencil between your teeth to avoid lip movements.

6. The perfection of techniques does not depend on how much practice you give them.

7. Fix your gaze on the centre of the space between lines 1 and 2.
8. The pencilled crosses will serve as focusing points for your gaze.
9. Do not trouble to time yourself as you carry out the two-line technique.
10. You need not set yourself the goal of discontinuing the mechanical aids.
11. Our aim is to concentrate on giving you guided practice in a single type of reading matter.
12. It is difficult to persuade a slow reader that he can increase his speed.
13. A really fast reader can read at four times the rate of a slow reader.
14. To remember a thing properly it is necessary to read it slowly.
15. To remember a thing properly it is necessary to read it fast.

Now check your answers against the answer key which you will find on page 159.

ANSWER KEYS TO COMPREHENSION TESTS
The Man Who Disturbed The Sleep Of The World
(*See* page 89)

1. (*c*); 2. (*a*); 3. (*b*); 4. (*c*); 5. (*a*); 6. (*a*); 7. (*a*); 8. (*b*); 9. (*a*); 10. (*a*).

Child Guidance Report
(*See* page 95)

1. (*a*); 2. (*b*); 3. (*c*); 4. (*b*); 5. (*a*); 6. (*b*); 7. (*c*); 8. (*b*); 9. (*a*); 10. (*a*).

Multiply your total of correct answers in each comprehension test by 10. This gives your score as a percentage and you can keep a record of it by entering it on the chart provided on page 160.

CHAPTER SEVEN

BEAT THE CLOCK AND GET THE IDEA

Comparing the reading speed of a fluent adult with that of a slow adult reader, C.H. Judd found that the fluent reader, in reading a paragraph containing 52 words, made 24 pauses in his eye movements. The slow reader, on the other hand, made twice that number. Moreover, the slow reader paused longer at each stop than the fluent reader.

Besides illustrating a point that was made much earlier in the book, this is clear evidence that slow reading is inefficient. It is such experiments as this which have led to the present-day widespread interest in individual differences in reading speeds.

In other psychological laboratories up and down the country the problem we are discussing has been investigated from various angles. For instance, at Loughborough College of Technology, Leicestershire, Miss Dyce-Sharp, Lecturer in Social Sciences, using groups of students and staff, has conducted experiments in which various methods of improving the rate of reading have been explored.

The reading processes of adults and the possibility of improving them have also been investigated by Professor M.D. Vernon in the Department of Psychology at the University of Reading. This experimental investigation was carried out with particular reference to the special courses of training held at the G.P.O. Headquarters, and a preliminary discussion of the topic was published by Professor Vernon in the *British Journal of Educational Psychology*.

The training of nurses, too, has been assisted by the results of such studies. For example, a group of student nurses who were slow readers were given practice in faster reading, using material on the history of nursing. They were asked questions to test their comprehension of what they read. At the end of the practice period all the students were found to have improved in their speed of reading. One student increased her reading rate by 55 per cent.

This experiment is reported by Dr Marian East Madigan in her *Psychology: Principles and Applications*.

Outside the walls of the psychological laboratory there has also been a considerable growth of interest in rapid reading and the benefits to be derived from it. For instance, U Thant, former secretary-general of the United Nations, subscribed to 25 or 30 newspapers every week, and got up at 6 a.m. every day in order to be able to read them all.

He was one of many millions of people whose need of rapid reading had been brought urgently to his notice. You, too, are one of this number and in this book I have already equipped you with some useful techniques to aid you towards achieving this end. In this chapter I propose to take you a step further and add two more techniques to your repertoire.

Beat the clock
1. '*Pacing*'. The first of these is 'pacing'. Pacing means setting yourself a time limit for the reading of a piece. This, of course, is governed by the number of words it contains and the faster pace at which you think you can read it.

For this purpose you are recommended to get a friend to time you with a stop-watch, if possible. Failing a stop-watch, an ordinary watch or clock will do.

The piece that follows contains 465 words. What reading speed have you achieved up to now? What speed do you think you can accomplish on the following passage, which consists of some general explanatory remarks on matters of health and diet?

Consult the Speed-Time Chart at the end of this chapter. Check the column headed 'speed'. Let your eye run up the column until you come to a speed which you think you are now capable of. Then read across to the right to find your time in column A.

Your aim in reading this passage should be to 'beat the clock'. You want to read at a speed which will enable you to finish the passage before the person who is timing you says: 'Time's up!'

This is a valuable piece of training for several reasons. One is that it introduces an element of competition into your practice. It is well known that when a person is set to compete against his own previous record he may do better than when he is competing against others.

Another reason is that the use of the 'pacing' method helps to give you an incentive. You are made to feel that you have a set task to perform and are 'on your toes' to see that you get through it in time. The question of motive is important in anything we undertake. In whatever we try to do we need to feel that we are doing it for a specific purpose, that we have a definite aim or goal in view.

Yet another reason is that 'pacing' serves as a definite indication of whether or not you have accomplished your task. You receive an immediate reward in the form of the knowledge that you have done what you set out to do. This reward reinforces your efforts and encourages you to do even better in the future.

Here is a reminder, then, about what 'pacing' expects from you. This technique is:

Set yourself a time limit for the reading of a piece according to the number of words it contains and the faster pace at which you think you can read it. Have someone time you by means of a stop-watch or otherwise. Try to beat your par. Have your friend call out when the time is up, while you try to finish reading the piece before he does so. Refer to the chart at the end of the chapter for reading speeds and times.

Are you ready to start reading? Has your friend noted the time within which you want to finish this passage, and is he ready to call out 'Time's up!' after the set interval has elapsed?

Practice Material – V

All right. Start to read *now*.

GENERAL HEALTH AND DIET RULES
The general rules of health and diet and the different ways of applying them should be carefully followed if you would attain that bodily and mental fitness that is so essential to success and happiness.

You must so live your life that your body is at least a well-fuelled machine, and you must treat its delicate machinery with the same respect as you would a gold watch. Fussiness is, of course, not recommended but you can, without being fussy, see that your body and its functions are properly treated, so that they are more responsive to the messages from the 'control room' – the brain.

You must rest sufficiently, taking about eight hours' sleep every night; sleep with your window open, except, of course, in foggy weather. Get plenty of fresh air and a certain amount of daily exercise: walking is the most natural and is very beneficial. A daily lukewarm bath is soothing to the nerves.

By following these simple general health principles, you will soon find that you will not tire so easily, and in the morning you will feel more energetic, and be ready to cope with the problems connected with your daily work.

To pay attention to one's diet is another secret of the attainment of vibrant health. Eat less than your usual amounts; do not eat too much meat; peas, beans and lentils will supply you with energy and nourishment.

Eat plenty of fresh fruit, raw for preference: oranges, lemons, grapefruit, dried apricots, apples, raisins, bananas. Take plenty of fresh vegetables and green leafy plants: watercress, lettuce, young onions, cabbage, carrots, runner beans, tomatoes.

Eat brown bread in preference to white. Porridge and other wholemeal foods, butter, cheese and eggs are good; honey may also be taken.

Besides giving attention to your diet, watch your habits during and after meals. If possible, sit for ten minutes after each meal; eat slowly and masticate your food thoroughly. Attend to the process of elimination, and do this by means of correct food and not with purgatives. If you do find these necessary for a time, use liquid paraffin.

Fruit juice is also excellent as a laxative; squeeze the juice of two or three oranges or lemons into a tumbler and drink first thing every morning. This will prove beneficial in more ways than one, for it will supply you with energy and vitality and it will help to purify the blood stream.

If you carry out these instructions you will feel a continuous increase in health. Of course, improvement is bound to be gradual, for there may be the effects of many years of bad habits to be overcome. Nevertheless, to attain vibrant fitness will be a great asset in becoming happy and successful in life.

Now stop reading. All you have to do next is to wait for your friend to tell you how far ahead of your set time you are. If you have succeeded in 'beating the clock' and you were not too modest in judging what speed you could accomplish, you have done well.

The important thing is that you have tested yourself. You have tried your strength, as it were, and from this experience you should have gained a useful impression of the extent to which your new-found rapid-reading skills are being consolidated. To put yourself to the test in this way is invaluable, because when you succeed it gives you added confidence in your powers and strengthens your resolve to continue on the path you are taking.

Don't be discouraged if the time elapsed before you had finished this passage. Maybe you were a trifle over-optimistic in assessing the level of difficulty of the passage. Maybe you thought it was a little easier than it turned out to be, or maybe you are not quite ready for the reading speed you wanted to attain. In any case don't worry, for I am going to give you quite a bit more practice with various kinds of materials before you get to the end of this book. Naturally, I also hope that you will not desist from your practice efforts even when you have finished the book. In your day-to-day reading I want you to go on practising the techniques which you are acquiring here, until you are entirely satisfied with the adequacy of your reading speeds to meet the demands of your business life or leisure hours.

You will notice that in the last sentence of the previous

paragraph I said 'reading *speeds*' and not 'reading *speed*'. This was done deliberately. It is likely that you will develop more than one new reading speed, so that you can readily and automatically adjust yourself to the demands of the different kinds of reading matter which you encounter from time to time.

But I shall have more to say on this subject later. For the moment I will just remind you of the usefulness of having more than one speed. Later on I will give you practice in adapting your speed to the level of difficulty of what you are reading – even when the level of difficulty varies within the same passage.

Britain's reading interests

When a national daily newspaper took a poll of Britain's reading interests, it was found that most people who read at all read *books* either occasionally or regularly. No more than about three out of ten people admitted to reading books only rarely or never.

Buying them and borrowing them from a library are the commonest methods by which people get hold of books. Only about two out of ten people borrow books from a friend and far fewer obtain them from a book club.

How are people influenced in choosing what they read? Reading itself is actually among the commonest methods that determine the choice of what to read. About six out of ten people read a particular book because of published reviews or because the author's name or subject is known to them. In other words, our reading choice is determined by the fact that we have previously read what somebody else thinks about a book or because we have read something else which the author has written or something else on the same subject by another author.

All this points to the cumulative effect of reading as a determinant of tastes and interests. The more we read the more catholic we can become in our tastes or the more knowledgeable in our outlook. But, because the span of life is limited, we can never read as much as we would like to, although we can make a conscientious effort to put to the utmost use the time that we have available for reading. This we can do by mastering the techniques of rapid reading which are being taught here.

Get the idea

2. *Go for the meaning.* So far I have given five of these techniques. Now let me turn to the next. To help you to succeed with this technique I want you to turn your attention partly away from what you are reading and to direct it to what is happening within you.

What is going on in your mind as you read? Are you saying the words to yourself? I hope not. I have already shown you a way of stopping the practice of actually mouthing the words as you read. Now I want you to get the meaning directly, without the intermediary step of repeating the words mentally. Can you do this? Perhaps not immediately but at least I know you are willing to have a good try.

Do you understand what I am driving at? I want you to go for meanings – not just for words. For instance, suppose you read:

Most nouns form their plural by adding -s to the singular.

What did you do? You fixed your eye on the word 'plural' and in one or two glances took in as many words as you could on either side of it. Am I right? But were you reading only *words*? What is the *meaning* of this sentence? The meaning can be expressed thus:

Noun – noun*s.*

This is the essential thought which you are required to get from the sentence. This is all you need in order to grasp its meaning. We can readily see from this example that mere words are not so very important after all, are they? They are only means to an end, the end being a meaning. If you get the meaning you can discard the words. The meaning can be embodied in your mental structure in the form of a picture of the letter -*s* which can be added to form the plural. If you can see this meaning in your mind you can apply it to all the numerous cases where it is relevant, i.e., to most English nouns.

You will agree that there is a significant difference between this and repeating mentally to yourself the words of the above sentence. So remember: it is the meanings you want from your reading – not just the words, although they, too, are important as the vehicle of meaning. But they are not an end in themselves.

Practice Material – VI
Apply this technique to the following passage. Try to see the meanings in your mind as you read it. Pay less attention to the words. You will still have to read the words, of course, but don't waste time repeating them over in your mind. Think of what the words mean – not so much of what the words actually are. Try to reconcile the meanings with what you already know, fitting them into the framework of the knowledge which you use in directing your affairs.

In reading the following passage I suggest that you don't bother to time yourself. Of course, it is still important that you should read at the fastest rate of which you are capable. But in this particular instance I want you to add something more. I want you to read with speed but also with comprehension of meanings, paying less attention than has been your custom to repeating the words to yourself in that 'inner speech' which slows down your reading speed.

Are you ready to start reading for the ideas implicit in the words of this passage, giving these ideas or meanings priority over the mere words which express them? If you are, off you go.

NOUNS IN THE PLURAL

When we name someone or something, the word that we use is a *noun*. Consider the following list of words: *boy, town, jug, practice, practise, indeed, beauty*. Of these words, *boy, town, jug, practice* and *beauty* are nouns, because they are names of someone or something. *Practise* and *indeed* are not nouns, because they are not the names of anything.

A noun can be the name of one person or thing, or it can be the name of more than one person or thing. For instance, *park* is the name of one thing: it is said to be a *singular* noun. On the other hand *melons* is the name of more than one thing: it is said to be a *plural* noun.

Most nouns form their plural by adding -s to the singular. If one turns to the dictionary, the nouns listed there will be found to be in the singular. Thus *habit* is the name of one settled tendency or practice. The name of more than one settled tendency or practice is *habits*, which is the plural of *habit*. To form the plural all that one does in the case of most nouns is to add *-s* to the singular form given in the dictionary.

You will notice that we said *most* nouns, not *all*, form their plural by adding *-s*. The fact that some nouns do not form their plural in this way is where the difficulty begins to creep in. However, we will consider each of the exceptions in turn, giving examples in the hope of making the matter clear.

First of all we have to deal with nouns which in the singular end in *-y*, like *lady, baby, monkey, delay*. If the letter in front of *-y* is a vowel (*a, e, i, o* or *u*), everything is straightforward: we simply add *-s* to the singular. Thus the plurals of *monkey* and *delay* are *monkeys* and *delays*. On the other hand, if *-y* is preceded by any letter other than a vowel, the rule is that we *change y into i and add -es*. Thus the plurals of *lady* and *baby* are *ladies* and *babies*, because in each noun *-y* is preceded by a letter other than *a, e, i, o*, or *u*.

Next there are nouns which already end in *-s* in the singular. Examples are *boss, gas, address*. Along with such nouns we may also group those ending in *-sh, -ch, -x* (except *ox*). *These nouns form their plural by adding -es.*Thus the plurals of *boss, gas, address, brush, church* and *box* are *bosses, gases, addresses, brushes, churches* and *boxes*.

Some nouns ending in *-o* also form their plural by adding *-es*. Examples are *potato* (*potatoes*), *hero* (*heroes*), *Negro* (*Negroes*). Other nouns ending in *-o* simply add *-s*. For instance, the plurals of *piano, studio, photo* are *pianos, studios, photos*. Note that *banjo* and *grotto* form their plurals in either way: *banjos* or *banjoes*; *grottos* or *grottoes*.

Note that the plural of some nouns is the same as the singular. Some nouns denoting animals, fish and birds fall into this class, e.g., *sheep, deer, salmon, trout, grouse*, and so on. Other nouns denoting fish, e.g., *shark, whale, herring, eel*, form their plural according to the usual rule, i.e., by adding -*s*.

Some nouns are used only in the plural, because their meaning does not permit of a singular. The nouns *pliers, tidings, tongs, entrails* have no singular.

It is a mistake to give the word *offspring* a plural form. *Offspring* means either one child or more than one child. Consequently there is no need to add an -*s* to the word. In any case, if a person were to say, 'I have several offspring,' he would be thought to be speaking in just a slightly joking fashion. If you want to be taken seriously, say, 'I have several children.'

Incidentally, I have used here a plural formed in a way different from any noted so far. There are just a few nouns whose plurals end in -*en*. Another is *ox* (*oxen*). Note that *brother* has two plurals. Ordinarily the plural is *brothers,* but when we refer to fellow members of a society, especially a religious one, the plural is *brethren.*

Another way of forming the plural is by changing the vowel sound of a word. Thus the plurals of *foot, goose, man, mouse, tooth* and *woman* are *feet, geese, men, mice, teeth* and *women.*

Further, we must note nouns which have more than one plural. In such cases the different plurals often have different meanings, as we observed with *brother.* For instance, *penny* has two plurals: *pence* and *pennies.* When we are thinking of their value, we use the former, e.g., 'Take care of the *pence* and the pounds will take care of themselves.' When we are thinking of the individual coins, the plural is *pennies,* e.g., 'He gave me my change all in *pennies.*'

A good dictionary is the best guide in ascertaining which plural is the correct one to use in a particular instance.

Finally, we must mention nouns which end in -*f.* Some of these form their plural in the normal way by adding -*s*, e.g., *chief* (*chiefs*), *dwarf* (*dwarfs*) *reef* (*reefs*). Others, however, drop the -*f* and add -*ves*, e.g., *wolf* (*wolves*), *leaf* (*leaves*), *calf* (*calves*), *loaf* (*loaves*). Note also *knife* (*knives*), *life* (*lives*). *Hoof* has both *hoofs* and *hooves,* but *roof* has only *roofs. Scarf,* too, has *scarfs* or *scarves.*

I have not said everything that might be said about the formation of the plural, but at least I have covered the main rules which will serve for all ordinary purposes. In cases of doubt, let me repeat: consult a reliable dictionary.

In reading this passage did you cut your 'inner speech' to a minimum? Did you try to stop yourself saying the words over in your mind and go for the meanings instead? Let us see, then, how well you have mastered the meanings. Take the following comprehension test and then check your answers by the key which will be found on page 111.

COMPREHENSION TEST
Nouns in the Plural

1. An example of a singular noun is:
   - (a) Melons.
   - (b) Beauty.
   - (c) Practise.
2. When a noun adds -*s* it is said to be:
   - (a) In the singular.
   - (b) In the dictionary.
   - (c) In the plural.
3. The formation of the plural is governed by:
   - (a) Only one rule.
   - (b) Several rules.
   - (c) No rules at all.
4. Nouns ending in -*y* change *y* into *i* and add -*es* when the *y* is preceded by a vowel. This statement is:
   - (a) True.
   - (b) False.
   - (c) Meaningless.
5. Nouns which end in -*s* form their plural
   - (a) By adding another -*s*.
   - (b) By adding -*es*.
   - (c) By remaining unchanged.
6. The plural of *gas* is:
   - (a) Gasess.
   - (b) Gases.
   - (c) Gasses.
7. The plural of *potato* is:
   - (a) Potato.
   - (b) Potatos.
   - (c) Potatoes.
8. An example of a noun which has more than one plural is:

(a) Penny.

(b) Hero.

(c) Reef.

9. The rule for forming the plural of nouns ending in -*f* is:

(a) They all add -*s* to the singular form.

(b) They all drop -*f* and add -*ves*.

(c) Some add -*s* while others drop -*f* and add -*ves*.

10. If you are in doubt about the plural of a word the best thing to do is to:

(a) Add -*s* to the word.

(b) Consult a good dictionary.

(c) Put what sounds best.

Turn to page 111 for the correct answers to these questions.

Subvocalizing

Subvocalizing means pronouncing the words silently to ourselves as we read them. The reader himself is, of course, aware that he is doing this, and, although it is not immediately obvious to anyone else, it can be detected by an outside observer. This can be done by electronic measurement of muscle potentials in the throat; these show that the words are being mouthed silently.

The habit is thought to originate from the exercise of reading aloud practised in schools. This also reduces reading speed in another way – by slowing down the movements of the eyes to the speed at which we speak.

Subvocalizing is not easy to get rid of. Progress in eliminating it, however, will come as you build up the habits of reading by lines or sentences instead of by single words. These habits are paths to the goal of grasping the meaning directly instead of merely reading the printed page.

A student said: 'If, when driving, I see a road sign with a right-angled triangle in black, I do not say silently to myself: Danger, steep hill. I know that is what the sign means by the look of it.' That is, he has gone for meaning instead of repeating words. You should do the same. Distil the essential thought from the words or other symbols that you read, and incorporate this in your mental structure by tying it up with what is already there.

Researchers in the United States have developed a method

of dealing with subvocalizing known as 'biofeedback training.' This is based upon using an instrument to measure the amount of movement in the reader's throat and giving him information or 'feedback' about how much there is. Monitoring his movement in this way puts him in a position to control it by relaxing and so reducing the amount of 'inner speech' that goes on while he reads.

'An annoying noise,' write David Boxerman and Aron Spilken in *Alpha Brain Waves* (Celestial Arts, 1975), 'sounds every time his throat muscles become active, while relaxing them will allow him to read in peace and quiet. Progress was quite rapid and reading speed improved noticeably.'

In the next chapter we go on to complete our study of the eight or so techniques for more rapid reading which this book offers you. Remember that in your regular reading you must, in order to develop the necessary skill, continue to practise the techniques which you have learned so far. Make the habits which they imply part of your daily routine and you will soon find that rapid reading becomes a natural skill in your business and professional life and in your spare-time activities.

SELF-TESTING QUIZ
Put a tick opposite the statements which you have read in Chapter 7.
1. The training of student teachers has been assisted by experimental reading studies.
2. The secretary-general of the United Nations subscribed to 60 newspapers every week.
3. In this chapter we add three more techniques to your repertoire.
4. Pacing means setting yourself a time limit for the reading of a piece.
5. Pacing introduces into your practice an element of competition with others.
6. The use of the pacing method helps to give us an incentive.
7. From pacing we receive an immediate reward in the form of the knowledge that we have done what we set out to do.
8. When you succeed it gives you added confidence in your powers.
9. Desist from your practice efforts when you have finished the book.
10. We envisage the likelihood of your developing only one new reading speed.

11. Most people who read at all read newspapers.
12. The more we read the less catholic we can become in our tastes.
13. If you get the meaning you can discard the words.
14. Sub-vocalizing is easy to get rid of.
15. There is no need to distil the essential thought from the words you read.

Now check your answers against the answer key which you will find on page 159.

ANSWER KEY TO COMPREHENSION TEST
Nouns In The Plural (*See* page 108)

1. (*b*); 2. (*c*); 3. (*b*); 4. (*b*); 5. (*b*); 6. (*b*); 7. (*c*); 8. (*a*); 9. (*c*); 10. (*b*).

Multiply your total of correct answers in each comprehension test by 10. This gives your score as a percentage and you can keep a record of it by entering it on the chart provided on page 160.

SPEED-TIME CHART
(*See* pages 99 and 112)

SPEED	TIME	
w.p.m.	mins.	secs.
1,200		23
1,100		25
1,000		28
900		31
800		35
700		40
600		47
500		56
400	1	10
300	1	33
200	2	20
Read up and across	A	

The first column gives reading speeds in words per minute. Column A gives the time required to read 'General Health And Diet Rules' (465 words) at the indicated speed.

Consult the first column for the desired speed and then read across for the appropriate time limit for the 'paced' reading passage in this chapter.

CHAPTER EIGHT

A CHANGE OF PACE
IS AS GOOD AS A REST

1. *Vary your pace*. The next technique of faster reading to which I want to introduce you is that of varying your pace according to need. Often it isn't necessary to read the whole of a piece of material at the same speed. The material may vary in difficulty from paragraph to paragraph or even within individual paragraphs, and the less difficult parts of it can be read more rapidly than the rest.

For example, consider the following passage:

WE SHOULD NOT HAVE PLAYS OF THE 17th AND 18th CENTURIES THRUST UPON US BY THE B.B.C.

The phrase 'plays of the 17th and 18th centuries' covers the works of dramatists who flourished between 1600 and 1799. The outstanding figure is Shakespeare, although not all of his plays are included in this period. Other noted dramatists of the period are Ben Jonson and Beaumont and Fletcher. The chief writers of the 17th-century Restoration drama are Dryden, Wycherley, Otway, Congreve, and Vanbrugh. With the end of Restoration drama came Gay's *Beggar's Opera* and the plays of Goldsmith and Sheridan.

Some arguments in favour of not having the plays of this period produced to-day by the B.B.C. are as follows:

1. The language in which they are written is not easy to understand. It employs words and constructions that have fallen out of use. Such plays are better adapted to being read at leisure, when the reader can consult notes elucidating the linguistic difficulties.

2. Many of the plays are written in poetic form, which is no longer suitable for the modern stage. It strikes an artificial note in the ears of the playgoer accustomed to prose dialogue.

3. The moral tone of some of the plays is offensive. This is true of some of the plays of Shakespeare, such as *Measure for Measure*. It is particularly true of the work of the Restoration dramatists. For example, discussing the plays of Dryden, a critic has said: 'The actions are often monstrous and revolting, the events not only improbable in themselves, but void of any artifice that should make them seem less improbable ... The events and their setting are hopelessly at variance.'

4. The above faults did not trouble an audience of courtiers, which sought only to be amused in its own way or at most to criticize on its own lines. However, the B.B.C. commands a much wider and more critical audience than this, and should respect the tastes of its listeners and viewers.

This passage is obviously not of the same level of difficulty throughout. The first paragraph, which is descriptive and introductory, is easier to read than the remaining paragraphs, which call for close attention to the thought. This is in spite of the fact that the first paragraph contains a longish list of proper names.

One might reasonably expect, therefore, to be able to get through the first paragraph at a faster pace than through the body of the argument. But even within the argument itself there are some sentences which are easier to read than others. For example, the ending of the third argument is easier to read than the beginning, because it does not add anything further to the thought but merely supports or illustrates it. In reading this paragraph, then, one might expect one's speed to increase towards the end of it.

Practice Material – VII

To modify one's speed according to the level of difficulty of the material is a useful technique to learn. In the passage that follows I want you to practise this technique deliberately. In this passage you will find that some paragraphs can be read more easily and quickly than others. I want you to work through these paragraphs at a faster pace than the others. By thus modifying your speed according to the difficulty of the material you add not only to the speed but also to the intelligence and discrimination with which you read.

For your convenience I have numbered the paragraphs. Please note that the following numbered paragraphs will probably be found easier to read than the rest. These paragraphs, then, should be read more rapidly.

3, 5, 7, 8, 11, 12, 16, 19.

To assist you further I have printed in italics the paragraphs in which I want you deliberately to increase your speed over and above the faster average speed which you are maintaining in reading this selected extract as a whole.

You need not bother to time yourself, but put into practice the techniques which you have learned for maintaining your speed in addition, when you come to one of the numbered paragraphs printed in italics, imagine yourself increasing your speed still further. You should find that you are able to do so without losing any of the meaning.

Start reading *now*.

DO WE LIVE HEREAFTER?

1. From earliest times man has in various ways answered this question for himself. The ancient Egyptians, for example, believed that when the body died, the soul was carried off to the underworld. Here in the realm of Osiris it was weighed in a balance against a peacock's feather. If through good deeds it had become refined and therefore lighter than the feather, it passed to the realms of eternal bliss. On the other hand, if it was weighted down with a load of evil deeds, it was condemned to eternal torment.

2. The ideas of the Romans about the future state of the soul were less colourful. For them the underworld or realm of Orcus was a place of gloom and sadness, and they built their tombs along the great highways so that the dead might be cheered by the sight of passers-by. The Hebrew underworld, too, is similar in character to the Roman Orcus – a dim place

of dust and decay known as Sheol.

3. *The Greeks, however, pictured their dead as living in the Elysian fields, of which the poet Virgil sings in his immortal* Aeneid. *This picture bears a close resemblance to the after life portrayed by our own poets, such as Tennyson, whose warrior departs to a blessed haven assuring him of immortality:*

> *'He passes to the Isle Avilion;*
> *He passes and is healed and cannot die.'*

Eat, drink and be merry

4. The idea behind the views presented here is that the body is survived by an immaterial essence or spirit. This idea, however, is by no means shared by all the thinkers of antiquity. The ancient philosopher Epicurus, for example, taught that the soul was composed of material atoms which perished at death and disappeared into oblivion. Hence he enjoined his followers to live for the day, for he believed that there was literally no to-morrow.

5. *Aristotle, the disciple of Plato and founder of the Peripatetic school of philosophy, taught that the thinking mind was the only eternal part of man. But he did not see in the possibility of its survival any grounds for postulating a personal immortality.*

6. Antiquity can provide us with some interesting, if not entirely acceptable, views of the nature of the life hereafter. Most readers will be interested, however, in the modern approach to the problem. Many enquirers have felt the need of some means whereby subjective beliefs could be corroborated or refuted by objective facts. In response to this need there has grown up the science of psychical research. This science includes in its field of enquiry the claim of spiritualism that, through the agency of trance mediums, it is possible to communicate with those who have 'passed over', and thereby to obtain information from which an acceptable and coherent account of life and conditions in the 'spirit world' can be pieced together.

7. *Some critics feel that the results of spiritualism are disappointing and that psychical research itself promises little better. The advantage of spiritualism, however, is that it offers the bereaved the consolation they*

seek. It appeals to those to whom solace is no less important than truth.

8. *Yet it is of some significance that in the whole period of its existence (since* 1882) *the Society for psychical Research, which was formed expressly for the purpose of submitting the claims of spiritualism to the test of the scientific investigation, has never proclaimed its acceptance of the spiritualistic hypothesis of psychic phenomena. The present opinion of the Society is that 'some, if not all, of the phenomena of spiritualism appear to have their origin in the ultra-conscious processes in the mind.'*

9. It used to be thought, for example, that automatic writing was the work of spirits in the world beyond the veil. The majority of mediums who practise this method believe that the hand is controlled by spirit guides manifesting on another plane of existence. It is now known, however, that the so-called spirit messages spring from no other source than the unconscious mind of the automatic writer; in fact, automatic writing is one of the pieces of evidence for the existence of this level of mental operation.

10. Sir Oliver Lodge left a sealed envelope to be opened on receipt of instructions from him intended to prove his survival. The test was so designed as to exclude the possibility of telepathy and other theories that account for alleged communications from the dead. Although Sir Oliver is said to have communicated through mediums, the instructions that would prove his survival have not been received and the envelope has remained unopened since 1942.

11. *That survival is a matter of belief rather than knowledge is admitted even in the spiritualistic ranks. 'Spiritualism, however acceptable to the multitude, is not a proven scientific fact,' wrote one of spiritualism's foremost mediums, Mrs. Eileen Garrett, to the editor of* Psychic News.

Facts versus revelation

12. *If we appeal to facts to settle the problem we are discussing, we are likely to come away empty-handed, since the facts are few and far between. The after life, however, is also the concern of religion, which makes a different kind of appeal – one which is based on revelation rather than on the scientific method of induction.*

13. The religion in which we are likely to be most interested

is Christianity, which describes the after life in terms of reward and punishment. The faithful are rewarded with eternal bliss in heaven, while the wretched sinner is condemned to eternal punishment in hell. This implies not only that we survive but that we retain our individuality. To suppose that one loses his personal identity would destroy the force of this teaching and render meaningless the whole Christian conception of a life hereafter.

14. The only book in the Bible which provides us with scenes of heaven is The Revelation of St John the Divine. Its famous description of heaven (Revelation 21-22) as the 'New Jerusalem' tells us that the holy city 'lieth foursquare' (Revelation 21, 16), surrounded by a high wall of jasper (Revelation 21, 18) with three gates of pearl on each side. It is built of pure gold adorned with precious stones. Through it flows 'a river of water of life, bright as crystal', beside which grows the tree of life, 'bearing twelve manner of fruits, yielding its fruit every month.'

15. On the other hand, there are plenty of references in the New Testament to hell. St Matthew records that both soul and body may be destroyed in hell (Matthew 10, 28). He asserts that 'whosoever shall say, Thou fool, shall be in danger of the hell of fire' (Matthew 5, 22). Those who do iniquity are to be cast into the furnace of fire, where there shall be weeping and gnashing of teeth (Matthew 13, 42).

16. *The teaching of the Christian religion from the point of view of eschatology is somewhat revolutionary, as indeed it is in other aspects. Not only does it postulate the survival of the soul, but it also promises that at the end of the world the soul will receive a new body. It thus advances a step further than any of the teachings which we have considered so far.*

17. The reader's innermost convictions about an after life must inevitably be based on an appeal to that faith which the sceptic spurns. It is difficult to preserve such faith intact in the face of contradictions. The chief obstacle to accepting it is the thought that a religion which preaches the love of God also preaches eternal damnation. Unless one is a mental contortionist, a person of very great faith, or a fool, it is difficult to believe without reservations.

18. However, lest it be assumed that the Christian religion is alone in preaching the resurrection of the body, it should be pointed out that this belief is also part of the teaching of the ancient Persian religion of Zoroastrianism. The Zoroastrian believed that the dead will be brought to life at the end of the world. This universal bodily resurrection will be followed by a judgment, in which the sheep will be separated from the goats and each will be rewarded according to the life he has lived on earth. This is followed by a period of spiritual reconstruction presided over by Ahura Mazda. The sun god, having vanquished Ahriman, who corresponds to the devil in Christian theology, will inaugurate a new world where happiness reigns supreme.

19. *In present-day thinking there is a tendency to conceive of heaven as a rewarding opportunity for service on a larger scale, and of hell as a spiritual state of alienation from God which is its own worst punishment. But perhaps we should give up as hopeless the attempt to describe conditions which in their very nature are bound to be indescribable, assuming, of course, that they exist at all.*

Now stop reading. The following comprehension test, which you are asked to take, is based on the paragraphs in italics, which you read more rapidly than the rest. We want to show you that your comprehension of this article is not affected by the added speed at which you read the italicised paragraphs. In spite of this you did not lose any of the meaning, as your results on this test should show.

Answer the following questions by ticking the right choice and then check your choices by turning to the answer key which is printed on page 130.

COMPREHENSION TEST
Do We Live Hereafter?
1. Where did the Greeks picture their dead as living?
   (a) In the realm of Osiris.
   (b) In the underworld of Orcus.
   (c) In the Elysian fields.

2. What poet wrote the *Aeneid?*
   (*a*) Tennyson.
   (*b*) Virgil.
   (*c*) Walt Whitman.
3. Complete the following quotation: 'He passes to the —— Avilion.' The missing word is:
   (*a*) Realm.
   (*b*) Warrior's.
   (*c*) Isle.
4. Who founded the Peripatetic school of Philosophy?
   (*a*) Aristotle.
   (*b*) Epicurus.
   (*c*) St John the Divine.
5. What is the advantage of spiritualism?
   (*a*) It offers consolation to the bereaved.
   (*b*) It proves that the soul survives death.
   (*c*) It encourages the practice of automatic writing.
6. Has the Society for Psychical Research accepted the claims of spiritualism?
   (*a*) Yes.
   (*b*) No.
   (*c*) The article doesn't tell us.
7. Who is Mrs Eileen Garrett?
   (*a*) The editor of *Psychic News*.
   (*b*) A leading spiritualistic medium.
   (*c*) A Christian theologian.
8. Religion appeals to:
   (*a*) Revelation.
   (*b*) Scientific method.
   (*c*) Prejudice.
9. What else besides the survival of the soul does Christianity promise?
   (*a*) That the soul will receive a new body.
   (*b*) That sinners will not be punished.
   (*c*) That all will be rewarded equally.
10. The tentative conclusion of this article is that:
    (*a*) It is possible to describe something which is indescribable.
    (*b*) It is impossible to describe something which is indescribable.
    (*c*) It is up to us to live our present lives and not bother about an after life.

Turn to page 130 for the correct answers to these questions.

Relaxez-vous
2. *You can afford to relax.* This is the final technique on which
your increased reading speed depends. You have done very
well to persist with your efforts so far, and if you have properly
mastered the foregoing seven techniques I am sure that what
you are going to learn now should not give you any trouble.

In the preceding technique I picked out paragraphs where it
was possible to speed up even beyond the high speed at which
you were reading the rest of the extract. Now remember this:
when you are reading at a rapid speed, as you should be doing
by now, you can also afford to slow down at times, especially
when the thought content of a paragraph demands it.

To slow down slightly when the need arises enables you not
only to reduce the chances of missing any of the meaning, but
it also has a psychological advantage. This is that it gives a
change in what you are doing. It enables you to relax
occasionally. In this way you can forestall any possible
tendency for reading to tire you out or to make you worried
lest you should be falling below standard.

Deliberately to slacken your pace of your own free choice
permits you to feel that you are not under any outside
compulsion. Moreover, it means you can speed up again with
a renewed sense of zest, feeling all the better for the slight
grace you have allowed yourself. This incentive will also be
strengthened by the knowledge that having slowed down
slightly has enabled you to avoid the risk of losing anything
important as far as the meaning of what you read is
concerned.

'I am just a bit sceptical,' said Mr M.J., 'about the real
advantages of fast reading. I can understand that in some
circumstances there may be advantages. But in the average
case would it not spoil the pleasure of reading? I think of
reading as like driving a car. I seldom drive merely to get to
my destination. I have indeed many business trips to make,
but I never drive at the maximum speed that the conditions
allow. I like to be able to relax enough to give some of my
attention to the beauties of nature.

'Even when I am reading for business purposes, I like to be
able to appreciate a carefully constructed sentence or a well-

turned phrase. Would speed reading leave time for this? I wouldn't like to spend time on improving my reading speed only to find that I had acquired an ability that in practice did not suit me.'

One must admit quite frankly that rapid reading is not for those who wish to pause and admire the structure of a sentence or the turn of a phrase. To achieve this, of course, you need to read slowly.

Sydney Piddington tells us that, when he and other Australians were captured by the Japanese in World War II, an officer advised them to take a book with them into Changi POW camp in Singapore. Piddington took Lin Yutang's *The Importance of Living*. He says that he deliberately read it slowly in order to savour its literary qualities, spending about two months on it altogether.

But it is surely better to read slowly because you choose to than because you have to. If you are a slow reader, you have to read everything slowly – even when your aim is not to appreciate the construction of sentences and phrases.

The advantage of rapid reading, then, is that it gives you a wider range of reading speeds from which to select the one that is best suited to your immediate purpose.

Practice Material – VIII
Therefore, in the following passage I want you to practise this technique – to give yourself the freedom of slackening off slightly when the need arises. Remember that you are doing this for three reasons:

1. To make sure that you lose none of the meaning.
2. To reduce any risk of building up tension as a result of high-speed reading.
3. To give you added zest to pick up speed again.

In adopting this technique you are behaving rather like the driver of a railway train. He knows that he has a strict time-table to adhere to. But there are stages in his journey where he must slacken speed to allow for the state of the track, signals against him, and so on. When these contingencies arise he modifies his speed to meet them. When they have passed he opens the throttle again and builds up his speed with renewed interest in maintaining the timing he is supposed to stick to. He also reduces any possible risk to the lives of the passengers that might come from ignoring these contingencies of track, signalling, etc.

In the following passage I have italicized the more difficult paragraphs where it will be expedient to 'slacken off' your speed a little, like the train-driver coming to a section of the track where special caution is necessary. In these paragraphs special caution is necessary to make sure that you get out all the meaning. Therefore, when you come to the italics ease off a bit. Just drop down slightly below the level of high-speed reading which is now becoming, or has already become, normal to you.

Again you need not time yourself unless you wish to do so. Start reading *now*.

SOVIET SCIENTIFIC RESEARCH

In a paper on 'Development of School Children's Interest in Handicraft Lessons', published in the Soviet journal *Voprosy Psikhologii*, I.M. Tsvetkov of the Yaroslav Pedagogic Institute says that 'handicraft lessons are intended to develop in junior school-children working skills and habits, love for work, respect for the working people, and readiness actively to participate in social work.'

What a far cry this is from the days when we ourselves were at school! Asked what we were doing as we laboured over the piece of carpentry or metal work in the school workshop, we should have said: 'Making something.' We never thought that we were developing 'working skills and habits'. And I wonder how many of us love work all the more for having done handicraft at school? Did it teach us to respect the honest labourer? Did it make us wish to contribute our labour to the betterment of society?.

Some of the older generation may have learned these things at school, but for many of the younger generation school has merely taught them to despise such things. The young person who loves work for work's sake is nowadays so rare as to be almost unknown. What young person on the threshold of his career imagines himself building a better society? Few if any think of themselves in this way. They are more interested in the tangible and personal rewards of work – the well-furnished home, the expensive car, the TV set, the washing machine, and so on. Perhaps the Soviet psychologist, although his views would be considered 'old-fashioned' by western standards, has something useful to teach to-day's generation after all.

(I.M. Tsvetkov. Development of school-children's interest in handicraft lessons. *Voprosy Psikhologii*, No. 5, 52-58.)

Although Lenin isn't usually regarded as a psychologist by western psychologists, another paper in *Voprosy Psikhologii* assures Russian psychologists that he cannot put a foot wrong in this field as well as in the field of dialectical materialism.

Commenting on the fiftieth anniversary of the publication of Lenin's *Materialism and Empiriocriticism*, which was observed by 'progressive public opinion all over the world,' N.S. Mansurov says that the work 'is of immense importance for further development of all progressive science, including materialist psychology.' He refers to the understanding of sensations by natural scientists of the last century as 'one-sided', but promises his readers that Soviet psychologists are 'on the ball' in correcting it.

'The interpretation of sensations in the light of dialectical materialism,' he concludes, 'leaves no ground for the various faulty assertions by the supporters of the "symbol-theory" and by the psychologists and philosophers who are still misguided by out-of-date conceptions.'

Thus clearly does the State lay down the official line on which a problem is to be tackled by the scientists who are working in the Soviet Union. Western psychologists are, of course, working on the same problem on entirely different lines, and even if they have heard of Lenin's work they certainly don't consider that it is relevant to their researches.

(N.S. Mansurov. 'Materialism and Empiriocriticism' and the problem of sensations. *Voprosy Psikhologii*, No. 3, 3-13.)

K.K. Platonov discusses 'Psychological problems of outer-space flight.' His paper is concerned with reducing these problems to some kind of order rather than with attempting to

solve them. He classifies the *general* problems as follows:
1. *The effect of outer-space flight conditions on the cosmonaut's mentality.*
2. *The engineering-psychology problems of the outer-space flight.*
3. *Personnel selection and training.*

This author also isolates the following *specific* problems:
1. *Human activity under zero-gravity conditions.*
2. *The effect of a dangerous situation and long isolation upon the emotional side of human activity.*

The following suggestions are offered 'for bringing the adverse influences to a minimum'; he advocates that special attention should be paid to:
1. 'Cabin rationalization'.
2. Special training of cosmonauts.
3. Their education in the spirit of high moral attitude to their duties.

This paper is of considerable topical interest and it illustrates how, together with other sciences, psychology is contributing to the effective mounting of outer-space projects.

(K.K. Platonov. Psychological problems of outer-space flight. *Voprosy Psikhologii*, No. 3, 56-65.)

From the outer-space flight we come down to earth with a paper by B.N. Pushkin examining problems in railway traffic control. *The author asks how the principles of cybernetics[1] can be applied to a study of the traffic controller's work. 'The control of train movements at the station,' he says, 'is considered as a feedback system, in which the station dispatcher fulfils the function of the regulator.' Here again we find the standardization of the worker's activities set up as an ideal to be pursued. The paper visualizes the possibility that 'the entire set of operations performed by the person engaged in railway traffic control can be fixed objectively.'*

In the west we call this time and motion study or work study and we see it as aiming at greater efficiency and increased production. In both east and west it is clearly applicable to numerous fields of human activity and types of occupations, and it must be especially valuable in the field of

[1] Cybernetics: the science of control and communication in animals and machines.

railway working, for in other countries, including our own, the railways are going through a crisis at the moment.

(B.N. Pushkin. Some psychological problems involved in the control of traffic on railways. *Voprosy Psikhologii*, No. 3, 66-77.)

A.G. Vishnepolskaya criticizes the view put forward in France that reading has no effect upon the learning of spelling. She presents some experimental results which show that reading may play an important part in acquiring proper spelling habits. By this it is not meant that reading leads to a general improvement of the ability to spell but rather to an improvement of the ability to spell specific words which have been read.

Examples of Russian words the spellings of which are cited in this paper are:

> *initsiativa* (initiative)
> *orientirovatsya* (to orient oneself)
> *dirizhabl'* (airship)
> *inzhener* (engineer)
> *kavaleriya* (cavalry)
> *ventilyator* (ventilator)
> *batal'on* (battalion)
> *kolossal'ny* (colossal)
> *shosse* (highway)
> *iod* (iodine)

I suppose that most of us think that many English words are difficult enough to spell. But even some of the hardest English words seem trivial in comparison with some of the easier Russian ones. The unfamiliar combinations of consonants tend to be off-putting to the English eye, but the fact remains that nowadays in institutes of higher education in this country students are engaged in learning Russian. Many of them indeed have been recommended to give it preference over German as a second foreign language. And with good reason too, for if we thought that Russia played little or no part in international affairs before World War II that opinion has been revised since. Indeed Russian must be regarded as the 'up and coming' foreign language on account of the importance of Russia's influence in world politics and her growing influence in cultural and economic activities.

Dr Vishnepolskaya's paper concludes: 'There is a constant interplay between reading and writing as regards their effect upon the learning of spelling. The words which have already been encountered by pupils as difficult spelling problems are better retained in memory and give a better spelling effect in subsequent writing exercises. The more the pupil writes and the more spelling difficulties he encounters (independent of whether they are solved by him in a proper way or not), the stronger is the normalizing influence of reading on his spelling habits.'

(A.G. Vishnepolskaya. The effect of reading practice on pupils' spelling. *Voprosy Psikhologii*, No. 3, 129-138.)

L.P. Grimak has hit upon an interesting way of studying the emotional reactions of parachutists during a jump. Five parachutists were hypnotised and given suggestions that they were making the parachute jump. He thus claims to have reproduced under hypnosis their emotional experiences during all stages of parachuting. The results of the experiment show that the parachutist's blood pressure increases and his pulse rate and breathing quicken. This is most noticeable in the waiting period before leaving the aircraft. As soon as the canopy opens during the drop these symptoms tend to decrease, although even after the parachutist has landed safely they still remain higher than they were to start with.

A criticism that might be made of this experiment is that the results are rather meagre considering the amount of effort spent in obtaining them, and that in any case they are somewhat obvious and might perhaps have been known even without the experiment. The experiment is chiefly interesting, however, for the ingenuity which it displays in methodology, and it illustrates the value of hypnosis as a means of reproducing simulated conditions which cannot be studied or which it may be inconvenient to study directly on the spot at the actual time when they are experienced.

(L.P. Grimak. Reproduction of emotional experiences of a parachutist in hypnosis. *Voprosy Psikhologii*, No. 3, 139-142).

Now stop reading.

Here is another comprehension test. This time testing you

on the passage as a whole, so that you can see for yourself whether or not your understanding has benefited by the technique of relaxation you have introduced into your reading. This technique should have helped your reading of both the more difficult paragraphs (*italicized*) and also the less difficult ones by ensuring that you returned to them with renewed zest and enthusiasm after the slight slackening off which you allowed yourself in the remaining paragraphs. .

Answer these questions, as before, by ticking the appropriate choice. Then check your answers by comparing them with the key which is to be found on page 130.

COMPREHENSION TEST
Soviet Scientific Research

1. What does N.S. Mansurov refer to as 'one-sided'?
   (a) Nineteenth-century scientists' understanding of sensations.
   (b) Handicraft lessons in junior schools in the Soviet Union.
   (c) Lenin's *Materialism and Empiriocriticism*.

2. K.K. Platonov's paper on problems of outer-space flight is chiefly concerned with:
   (a) Attempting to solve such problems.
   (b) Reducing the problems to some kind of order.
   (c) Assessing which of the problems is least important.

3. The science of control and communication is:
   (a) Politics.
   (b) Dialectical materialism.
   (c) Cybernetics.

4. 'The control of train movements at the station is considered as a —— system.' The missing word is:
   (a) Moral.
   (b) Feedback.
   (c) Parachuting.

5. A.G. Vishnepolskaya's paper on spelling criticizes views put forward in:
   (a) France.
   (b) England.
   (c) America.

6. The Russian word for 'ventilator' is:
   (a) *Ventylator*.
   (b) *Ventilyator*.
   (c) *Ventilatyor*.

7. Does Dr Vishnepolskaya think that reading is an aid to spelling?
   (a) Yes.
   (b) No.
   (c) She was unable to conclude for lack of sufficient evidence.
8. The paper on the emotional experiences of parachutists is by:
   (a) I.M. Tsvetkov.
   (b) B.N. Pushkin.
   (c) L.P. Grimak.
9. How were the emotional reactions of parachutists studied?
   (a) By the experimenter himself dropping with them.
   (b) By giving them suggestions under hypnosis.
   (c) By inviting them to fill in questionnaires after making a drop.
10. In what does the particular interest of this piece of research lie?
    (a) In the novelty of its methodology.
    (b) In the originality of its results.
    (c) In the new light it throws on the effects of hypnosis.

Turn to page 130 for the correct answers to these questions.

SELF-TESTING QUIZ

Put a tick opposite the statements which you have read in Chapter 8.
1. It is always necessary to read the whole of a piece of material at the same speed.
2. The material may vary in difficulty from paragraph to paragraph.
3. To modify one's speed according to the level of difficulty of the material is a useful technique.
4. Your comprehension is affected by the added speed at which you read the italicized paragraphs.
5. You can afford to relax.
6. To slow down slightly when the need arises gives us a change from what we are doing.
7. We can forestall any possibly tendency for our reading to tire us out.
8. Deliberately to slacken our pace obliges us to feel that we are under an outside compulsion.
9. We can speed up again with a renewed sense of zest.
10. For relaxation you go to the easy, lighter type of reading matter.
11. You will not find that the principles described in this book are applicable to every class of reading.
12. A widespread belief in the usefulness of repetition has influenced educational practice for centuries.

13. You can see your reading speed go up as you continue to apply these techniques.
14. In this age of scientific miracles we are still reading with techniques of Victorian times.
15. Parents can help children to improve their reading skill.

Now check your answers against the answer key which you will find on page 159.

ANSWER KEYS TO COMPREHENSION TESTS
Do We Live Hereafter?
(*See* page 119)

1. (*c*); 2. (*b*); 3. (*c*); 4. (*a*); 5. (*a*); 6. (*b*); 7. (*b*); 8. (*a*); 9. (*a*); 10. (*b*).

Soviet Scientific Research
(*See* page 128)

1. (*a*); 2. (*b*); 3. (*c*); 4. (*b*); 5. (*a*); 6. (*b*); 7. (*a*); 8. (*c*); 9. (*b*); 10. (*a*).

Multiply your total of correct answers in each comprehension test by 10. This gives your score as a percentage and you can keep a record of it by entering it on the chart provided on page 160.

CHAPTER NINE

PRACTICE MATERIAL

This chapter is devoted entirely to practice. I will teach you no new techniques but want you to practise the ones you already know. I introduce a departure here by giving you material of a type which you have not had before, in fact several new types of material. The techniques you have learned so far are all applicable to these types of material, which should add to your interest and give you a more adequate idea of the scope of high-speed reading techniques and the wide variety of fields in which they can be applied.

Before you start to practise these selections let me briefly summarize the techniques which you have learned so far. They are as follows:

1. Aim at reading as much of one line at a time as you can.
2. Cut out looking back at previous lines.
3. Suppress unwanted lip, head and finger movements.
4. Try to take in the thought content of two lines at a time.
5. Try to finish the reading of a piece within a time limit.
6. Try to get the meaning without repeating the words mentally.
7. Quicken your pace according to the level of difficulty of the material.
8. Slacken your pace when it is necessary to do so.

Have you a sound grasp of all these techniques? You should by now have understood how they work and given yourself a fair amount of practice in using them. Now let us apply them to some common types of reading material which so far have not figured in this book. They are: some mathematical material, a schoolgirl's essay, a chemistry student's notes, and the annual report of a building society.

Practice Material – IX
This passage contains 515 words. Time yourself as you read it rapidly. Make a note of your time and then consult the Time-Speed Chart (see page 145) to work out your reading speed. Try to maintain or improve the level which you have achieved with the help of the techniques taught in this book. Remember to give attention to understanding what you read as well as to reading it faster.

HOW TO EXTRACT A SQUARE ROOT

The square root of a number is that number which when multiplied by itself yields the given number.

For example, the square root of 36 is 6, because 6 x 6 = 36.

The sign of the square root is $\sqrt{}$. Thus the square root of 36 is written $\sqrt{36}$.

To extract the square root of a number carry out the following steps:

1. Mark off the digits of the number, e.g., 2086·6624, in pairs, working to left and right of the decimal point, i.e., 20,86·66,24.
2. Take the first pair, i.e., 20, and find a number which when squared, i.e., multiplied by itself, yields the given number or a lesser number nearest to it, i.e., 4 x 4 = 16.
3. Subtract 16 from 20, leaving 4. Bring down the second pair, i.e., 86, making 486. This is the second dividend, i.e., the second number to be divided.
4. Double the first figure in the answer, i.e., 4 x 2 = 8, and bring down 8 as the first figure of the second divisor, i.e., the second number that divides.
5. Now find a number which when added after 8 and when the new number thus formed is multiplied by it will divide into the second dividend, i.e., 486. This number is 5, i.e., 85 x 5 = 425.
6. Subtract 425 from 486, leaving 61. Bring down the third pair of digits in the original number, i.e., 66, making 6166. This is the third dividend.

7. Now double the figures in the answer, i.e., 45 x 2 = 90. Bring down 90 as the first two figures of the third divisor.
8. Find a number which when added after 90 and when the new number thus formed is multiplied by it will divide into the third dividend, i.e., 6166. This number is 6, i.e., 906 x 6 = 5436.
9. Subtract 5436 from 6166, leaving 730. Bring down the fourth pair of digits in the original number, i.e., 24, making 73024. Use this as the fourth dividend.
10. Double the figures in the answer, i.e., 456 x 2 = 912. Use 912 as the first three digits of the fourth divisor.
11. Now find a number which when added after 912 and when the new number thus formed is multiplied by it will divide into the fourth dividend, i.e., 73024. This number is 8, i.e., 9128 x 8 = 73024.
12. As there is no remainder when 73024 is subtracted from 73024 this completes the calculation.

The working may be set out as follows:

$$
\begin{array}{r}
4\ 5 \cdot\ 6\ 8 \\
4)\overline{20,86 \cdot 66,24} \\
16 \\
85\quad 486 \\
425 \\
906\quad 6166 \\
5436 \\
9128\quad 73024 \\
73024 \\
\cdots\cdots
\end{array}
$$

Answer: $\sqrt{2086 \cdot 6624} = 45 \cdot 68$

We can check the accuracy of the answer by multiplying 45·68 by itself, when we should get the original number 2086·6624.

```
    45·68 x
    45·68
   365 44
  2740 8
 22840
18272
208666 24
```

Inserting the decimal point gives us 2086·6624.

Here is another example: Find the square root of 1·053 correct to three places of decimals.

Working:

```
        1· 0  2  6  1
     1)1·05,30,00,00
       1
       -
 202 ·  0530
        404
2046    12600
        12276
20521   32400
        20521
        11879
```

Answer correct to three places of decimals: $\sqrt{1\cdot053} = 1\cdot026$.
Check on accuracy:

```
    1·026 x
    1·026

    6 156
   20 52
 1 026 0

1·052 676
```

Practice Material – X
This schoolgirl's essay contains 580 words. Time yourself as
you read it rapidly. Make a note of your time and then consult
the Time-Speed Chart to work out your reading speed. Try to
maintain or improve the level of reading skill which you have
achieved with the help of techniques taught in this book.
Remember to give attention to understanding what you read
as well as to reading it faster.

CHAUNTECLEER AND PERTELOTE ON DREAMS
A sixth-form schoolgirl's essay

Chaucer's Nun's Priest shows us in his tale of Chauntecleer a
'gentil cok' who had seven mates, the fairest of whom was
Pertelote. Chauntecleer and Pertelote are sitting side by side
on a perch in a poor widow's 'halle'. Chauntecleer groans and
his mate demands to know the reason for such behaviour.

He replies that he has had a dream in which he saw a beast
that was like a hound.

> 'His colour was bitwixe yelow and reed,
> And tipped was his tayl and bothe his eeris;
> His snowte smal, with glowynge eyen tweye.'

This beast – a fox – had frightened him and made him
groan.

Pertelote is indignant and says that she cannot love a
coward who is frightened by a fox, but she gives him some
homely advice. His dream, she says, was evidently caused by
melancholy; the best thing, therefore, is to take a laxative, and
she herself will teach him how to use herbs for the purpose.
Before taking the laxative, however, he is to have some worms
to assist his digestion.

Chauntecleer thanks her for the advice but still considers
that dreams are significant, and then goes on to relate the
story of a dream as follows:

Two men went on a pilgrimage and arrived at a certain
town. They could discover no place in which to stay together
for the night, so, parting company, each went to whatever
lodging he could find. One slept in a stall, 'in a yeerd with

oxen of the plough'; the other was more fortunate – he 'was logged wel ynough.' During the night the latter had a terrible dream. He dreamed that his comrade asked him for help, saying that he was going to be murdered in the stall, and that his body would be buried in a cart of manure outside the town.

In the morning the body was found.

> 'And in the myddel of the dong they founde
> The dede man, that mordred was al newe.'

Chauntecleer follows this up with another story, which is also about two men. One of them dreamed that a man stood by his bed-side and warned him not to go on a projected voyage – if he did he would be drowned. The next day the man told his dream to his friend, but the latter took no notice of it and set out on the voyage.

The warning proved to have been justified, for

> '... casuelly the shippes botme rente,
> And shipe and man under the water wente.'

Then Chauntecleer, who is a great student, quotes instances of dreams famous in history and legend, and says, moreover, that he will have nothing to do with laxatives, for 'they been venymes'. And so he changes the subject of conversation.

The discussion between the two birds throws light upon their respective characters. Pertelote is full of common sense, and sceptical with a robust contempt for dreams and, apparently, for those who believe in their significance. Her education is limited and she can quote only from the popular 'Catoun', whose aphorisms would be known to every school child.

Chauntecleer has far more imagination and is consequently a prey to morbid fears. He can quote from the classics as well as from the Bible to support his contentions. His tactful 'translation' of 'mulier est hominis confusio' speaks volumes for his wife's ignorance and his own resource. This resource was to stand him in good stead later on.

Practice Material – XI
These student's notes contain 600 words. Time yourself as you read them rapidly. Make a note of your time and then consult the Time-Speed Chart to work out your reading speed. Try to maintain or improve the level of reading skill which you have achieved with the help of the techniques taught in this book. Remember to give attention to understanding what you read as well as to reading it faster.

LABORATORY PREPARATION OF SALTS

A. *Definition.*
A salt is a compound in which the hydrogen of an acid has been replaced by a metal.

B. *Types of salts.*
1. *Normal.* A normal salt is one in which the whole of the hydrogen of an acid has been replaced.
2. *Acid.* An acid salt is one in which only part of the hydrogen of an acid has been replaced.

Na_2SO_4 (*normal*)
$NaHSO_4$ (*acid*)

C. *Points to consider.*
1. Is the salt soluble in water?
2. Does it contain water of crystallization?
3. Is it decomposed by moderate heat?

D. *General methods.*
1. *Titration.* Take the soluble hydroxide of a metal and divide it into two parts. Using an indicator, titrate one part with the correct acid solution. Note the amounts and neutralize the second part of the base without indicator. Evaporate to dryness, if possible, or set aside to crystallize. Remove crystals and dry with white blotting-paper. For bisalts double the amount of acid.

$NaOH+HCl=NaCl+H_2O$
$Zn(OH)_2+2HCl=ZnCl_2+2H_2O$

2. *Neutralization of acid.* Take metal, metallic oxide, hydroxide, or carbonate of metal required and add it in small portions to the correct acid until the acid is used up. Filter and evaporate to dryness or set aside to crystallize.

$$Zn+2HCl=ZnCl_2+H_2$$
$$Zn+H_2SO_4=ZnSo_4+H_2$$
$$ZnO+2HCl=ZnCl_2+H_2O$$
$$CuO+H_2SO_4=CuSO_4+H_2O$$
$$Ca(OH)_2+2HNO_3=Ca(NO_3)_2+2H_2O$$
$$2KOH+H_2SO_4=K_2SO_4+2H_2O$$
$$CuCO_3+H_2SO_4=CuSO_4+H_2O+CO_2$$

3. *Precipitation.* This applies to salts which are insoluble or nearly so in water. Take a soluble salt of the metal and a soluble salt of the acid and add one to the other. Filter the precipitate and wash continuously till washings fail the tests for other salts formed or used. Dry in an oven at about 120°C. and then remove from filter paper. This method may be applied when all salts are soluble if the solubility varies considerably.

$$Na_2SO_4+BaCl_2=2NaCl+BaSO_4\downarrow$$
$$Ca(ClO_3)_2+2KCl=CaCl_2+2KClO_3\downarrow$$
$$AgNO_3+NaCl=NaNO_3+AgCl\downarrow$$

4. *Direct combination.*

   (a) Pass gas over metal.
   $$2Na+Cl_2=2NaCl$$
   $$Zn+Cl_2=ZnCl_2$$
   (b) Heat solids and drive away excess.
   $$Zn+S=ZnS$$
   $$Cu+S=CuS$$
   $$Fe+S=FeS$$
   (c) Basic oxide plus acidic oxide
   $$SiO_2+2NaOH=Na_2SiO_3+H_2O$$

E. *Specific methods.*

   1. *Ammonium salts.* These are easily prepared by adding an excess of NH_4OH to, or passing an excess of NH_3 into, the correct acid. Then boil off the excess of the

gas and a pure solution of salt remains. As ammonium salts are decomposed by heat the solution is only partly evaporated and set aside for crystallization. The crystals are then removed and dried.

$$2NH_4OH+H_2SO_4=(NH_4)_2SO_4+2H_2O$$
$$NH_4OH+HNO_3=NH_4NO_3+H_2O$$
$$NH_4OH+HCl=NH_4Cl+H_2O$$

2. *Bicarbonates*. Saturate the correct thydroxide or soluble salt of the metal with CO_2. Allow to evaporate. Alkali bicarbonates separate out, others change to normal carbonates. Only bicarbonates of K and Na have been separated as solids.

$$Na_2CO_3+H_2O+CO_2=2NaHCO_3$$

3. *Carbonates*. Pass CO_2 into soluble salt till saturated. Evaporate to dryness and then heat, when the pure carbonate is obtained.

$$2NaOH+CO_2=Na_2CO_3+H_2O \qquad (1)$$
$$Na_2CO_3+H_2O+CO_2=2NaHCO_3 \qquad (2)$$
$$2NaHCO_3=Na_2CO_3+H_2O+CO_2 \qquad (3)$$

4. *Bisulphites*. Saturate the correct hydroxide with SO . Only bisulphites of alkali metals have been obtained as solids.

$$NaOH+H_2SO_3=NaHSO_3+H_2O$$
$$2NaOH+H_2SO_3=Na_2SO_3+2H_2O$$

5. *Sulphites*. Saturate hydroxide with SO . Boil the solution and concentrate, when normal sulphite will crystallize. All bicarbonates and bisulphites are soluble in water.

$$NaOH+H_2SO_3=NaHSO_3+H_2O$$
$$NaHSO_3+NaOH=Na_2SO_3+H_2O$$

Practice Material – XII
This company report contains 1,030 words. Time yourself as you read it rapidly. Make a note of your time and then consult the Time-Speed Chart to work out your reading speed. Try to maintain or improve the level of reading skill which you have achieved with the help of the techniques taught in this book. Remember to give attention to understanding what you read as well as to reading it faster.

COMPANY REPORT

In his Annual Report Mr G. Fraser-Elphinston, Chairman of the Consolidated Building Society Ltd., referred to the satisfactory financial position for the year 19—. In the course of his speech at the 76th Annual General Meeting, held at the Society's headquarters office on 2nd May, the Chairman said:

This year the Society's assets have shown an increase of $9\frac{1}{4}$ per cent over the total figure for the corresponding period last year. Thus 19— may be put down as another record year in the Society's long and honourable history. It reflected the continued confidence of the public in its financial standing and the continued success of the Society in attracting new investment.

During the year the Society had lent a total of nearly £6 million, the bulk of which was borrowed in the form of mortgages taken out by owner-occupiers. The provisions of the latest Rent Act had drawn the attention of many more people to the advantages of owning their own homes, and as a consequence the Society's mortgage business had flourished on a very encouraging scale.

The Society had also attracted many new investors who saw in a Consolidated Building Society account a convenient way of saving at an attractive rate of interest. Although the Bank Rate had shown a tendency to fall during the year, the Society had done its utmost to offer adequate rates of interest, and the success of its policy had been seen in the annual turnover of investment shares and deposit accounts.

These figures have not been achieved by resting on the laurels which the Society had earned in the past. Hard work had been necessary to maintain prestige in a highly competitive field, but thanks to the loyalty of all branches of the Society the extra effort had proved well worth while. It was the Chairman's confident hope and expectation that if this hard work and determined effort continued in the year ahead, it would bring even greater justification for the policy of progressive development which had been pursued in the past.

The level of taxation in the economy generally continued to be a cause of misgiving in all quarters. This was a burden which had to be frankly acknowledged and the problem it created boldly faced. Nevertheless the Society looked forward to the possibility that there might be an easing of profits tax in the near future. In the meantime it would do its best to support those who were conducting an enlightened campaign for a reduction in the level of taxation generally, which it was felt was a check on the expansion of the Society's interests.

As a result of its merger with the North-Eastern Permanent Building Society, the Consolidated Building Society had acquired new premises in —. Expansion had also been necessary in a number of branch offices, and those at — and — had been considerably enlarged to accommodate the volume of new business coming to those branches in consequence of the local authorities' active building programmes in the areas in question. Extensive new estates of houses in the £14,000-£15,000 class had also been put up by private building concerns, and the Chairman was pleased to say that the Society's branches had also participated to its full share in the mortgage demand thus created.

It was with regret that he recorded the death on 27th October last of Major-General A. Annakin-Beazley, M.C., a respected member of the Board of Directors. Major-General Annakin-Beazley had been associated with the Society for a large number of years, and it would be recalled with appreciation that he had been an ardent advocate from the very first of the Society's expansion policy. He had lived to see it bear fruit but would be sadly missed in future.

His place on the Board of Directors had been filled by the appointment of Mr Walter G. Arbuthnot, who had been formerly General Manager of the Society's Southern Area branches. Mr Arbuthnot had had a long and varied experience with the Society, and in offering him this appointment it was felt that his experience would be an invaluable asset to the Board and also some overdue recognition of his years of valued service to the Society.

During the year the Society had formed a subsidiary, with a share capital of £188,000, for the exploitation of investment interests which the Society had acquired as a bequest under the terms of the will of the late Mrs Cordelia Lane, whose husband had been active for the Society in a managerial

capacity up to his own death in 19—. Mrs Lane's bequest
would be used for judicious investment in stocks and shares in
promising fields of new endeavour. The Board had thoroughly
discussed the choice of suitable preference stocks for this
purpose, and it had been decided that the best prospect of
capital gains was offered in industrial shares in certain of the
Common Market countries. Preliminary reports showed that
confidence in this subsidiary activity was fully justified by the
financial returns, which were of the order of 18-20 per cent for
the short period that the subsidiary company had been in
operation.

*Your Directors, therefore, venture to consider that the overall picture is
entirely satisfactory and places the Society in a very favourable position
for next year's operations. In moving the adoption of this Report I feel
that we have just cause to congratulate all concerned in maintaining our
financial position and effecting the highly gratifying improvement which
our figures have shown over the preceding year. My colleagues and I
retain our unshaken confidence in the assured future of the Society,
forming as it does an integral part in the welfare of the country as a
whole.*

After discussion the Report and Accounts were adopted. A
full copy may be obtained by interested persons by writing to
the Head Office, Sir Francis Drake Square, Stanby-on-
Humber, Yorks.

COMPREHENSION TEST
Practice Materials – IX-XII

1. What is the square root of a number?
   (a) The product of multiplying a number by itself.
   (b) That number which when multiplied by itself yields the
        given number.
   (c) Any number which can be divided by 2.

2. The square root of 36 is written
   (a) $\sqrt{36}$
   (b) $2\sqrt{36}$
   (c) 36 x 36

3. The extraction of the square root of a number can be checked by
   (a) Dividing the square root by 2.
   (b) Multiplying the square root by itself.
   (c) Subtracting the square root from the original number.

4. Chauntecleer and Pertelote are:
    (a) A man and his wife.
    (b) A cock and a hen.
    (c) Two men who went on a pilgrimage.
5. Who told the tale of Chauntecleer and Pertelote?
    (a) 'Catoun'.
    (b) The fox.
    (c) The Nun's Priest.
6. Where was the murdered man's body found?
    (a) Lying in a poor widow's 'halle'.
    (b) Buried in a manure cart.
    (c) Floating on the sea.
7. What types of salts are there?
    (a) Normal and acid.
    (b) Normal and abnormal.
    (c) Metallic and non-metallic.
8. When an acid is neutralized by a base the result is
    (a) A salt and water.
    (b) A gas and solid.
    (c) A metal and hydrogen.
9. Are ammonium salts decomposed by heat?
    (a) We are not told.
    (b) Yes.
    (c) No.
10. The Chairman's Annual Report deals with the activities of
    (a) A moral welfare society.
    (b) A temperance society.
    (c) A building society.
See below for the correct answers to these questions.

SELF-TESTING QUIZ

Put a tick opposite the statements which most nearly apply to yourself.
1. My reading speed is now about 250 words per minute or less.
2. My reading speed is now between 250 and 500 words per minute.
3. My reading speed is now between 500 and 800 words per minute.
4. My reading speed is now more than 800 words per minute.
5. My scores on the comprehension tests have averaged four correct answers or less.

6. My scores on the comprehension tests have averaged between five and eight correct answers.
7. My scores on the comprehension tests have averaged more than eight correct answers.
8. I find that I usually make more than six mistakes on the self-testing quizes.
9. I find that I usually make between three and six mistakes on the self-testing quizes.
10. I find that I usually get 100 per cent or nearly 100 per cent correct answers on the self-testing quizes.
11. I am disappointed with the progress which I have made so far.
12. I have made some progress but I think that I should have made more.
13. I am satisfied that I have made reasonable progress and I am looking forward to continuing to do so.
14. I feel that I have made very good progress.
15. I am highly satisfied with the progress which I have made.

Now check your answers against the answer key which you will find on page 159.

ANSWER KEY TO COMPREHENSION TEST
Practice Materials – IX-XII
(*See* pages 142-143)

1. (*b*); 2. (*a*); 3. (*b*); 4. (*b*); 5. (*c*); 6. (*b*); 7. (*a*); 8. (*a*); 9. (*b*); 10. (*c*).

Multiply your total of correct answers in each comprehension test by 10. This gives your score as a percentage and you can keep a record of it by entering it on the chart provided on page 160.

TIME-SPEED CHART

To find your reading speed in words per minute read upwards in the appropriate column until you locate your time or approximate time and then read across to the right-hand column.

Read up in appropriate column for time and across to end column for reading speed. For appropriate column see page opposite.

TIME								SPEED
min.	sec.	min.	sec.	min.	sec.	min.	sec.	w.p.m.
2	35	2	54	3	00	5	09	200
2	17	2	35	2	40	4	35	225
2	04	2	19	2	24	4	07	250
1	52	2	07	2	11	3	45	275
1	43	1	56	2	00	3	26	300
1	35	1	47	1	51	3	10	325
1	28	1	39	1	43	2	56	350
1	23	1	33	1	36	2	45	375
1	17	1	27	1	30	2	35	400
1	13	1	22	1	25	2	25	425
1	09	1	17	1	20	2	17	450
1	05	1	13	1	16	2	10	475
1	02	1	10	1	12	2	04	500
	59	1	06	1	09	1	58	525
	56	1	03	1	06	1	52	550
	54	1	01	1	03	1	48	575
	52		58	1	00	1	43	600
	50		56		58	1	39	625
	48		54		55	1	35	650
	46		52		53	1	32	675
	44		50		51	1	28	700
	43		48		50	1	25	725
	41		46		48	1	22	750
	39		44		45	1	17	800
	36		41		42	1	13	850
	34		39		40	1	09	900
	33		37		38	1	05	950
	31		35		36	1	02	1,000
	29		33		34		59	1,050
	28		32		33		56	1,100
	27		30		31		54	1,150
	26		29		30		52	1,200
A		B		C		D		SPEED

KEY TO TIME-SPEED CHART

Column A – How To Extract A Square Root (515 *words*).
Column B – Chauntecleer And Pertelote On Dreams (580 *words*).
Column C – Laboratory Preparation Of Salts (600 *words*).
Column D – Company Report (1,030 *words*).

CHAPTER TEN

HOW TO REMEMBER WHAT YOU READ FASTER

Can we remember better what we read faster? This question is really three questions, because there are three aspects of remembering. There is memorizing what we read, and there is recalling, reproducing or recognizing it afterwards. In between there is a third aspect. This is the retention of what we read in our brain cells. These three stages of the remembering process, i.e., recording, retaining and recalling, are the three R's of memory.

Thus, when we ask how we can remember better, we are asking: (1) How can we memorize better?; (2) How can we retain better?; and (3) How can we recall better? In practice we ignore the second question, because there is no way of actually improving the brain's sheer power of retention. The practical problem of memory concentrates on memorizing and recalling better.

How, then, can we memorize better in spite of having read faster? How can we recall better what we have read faster? In order to answer these two questions we must first examine what causes us to forget at all. When we know this we shall be in a stronger position to suggest how such causes might be overcome.

Forgetting: Causes
We forget something we have read because something else we have read interferes with it. This may be either something which we have read before or something which we have read after reading the forgotten item. In the latter case the interference is known as 'retroactive inhibition'; in the former case it is known as

'proactive inhibition'.

There are also more obvious causes of forgetting, such as lack of attention, insufficient repetition, lack of interest, and failure to form associations between what we read and what we know already. Lack of attention was dealt with in Chapter 2, How To Concentrate; the other three factors will be considered below along with the first two.

1. *Retroactive inhibition.* This means that the memory traces of subsequent experiences interfere with the memory trace of the experience we wish to remember. For instance, if we read a news item and then read a short story, the memory of the short story may interfere with the memory of the news item. We forget the latter because of the effect of retroactive inhibition from the former.

This operates in regard to all three aspects of remembering. The above example shows how it operates at the level of memorizing or recording the information contained in the news item. But retroactive inhibition also affects the ability to retain material in mind and the ability to recall it when needed.

For example, it seems likely that memory traces are laid down in our brain in the form of 'circuits', partly chemical and partly electrical in nature. A circuit formed by a later experience may interfere with one formed by an earlier experience. An analogy that will help in grasping the point is that of the aircraft passing overhead which disturbs the picture on our TV screen. This is retroactive inhibition at the level of retention.

Again, we are trying to recall something and a stray, unwanted thought crosses our mind. It breaks up the train of thought that we are pursuing in quest of some wanted item. This is retroactive inhibition at the level of recall.

Recent research has discovered two kinds of storage of memory traces in the brain: temporary and permanent. During temporary storage, an impression is liable to be erased although, even when in permanent storage, it can still be temporarily forgotten. Temporary storage appears to be made by means of a system of signals travelling round the neurones. After about an hour, either the memory trace is erased or the memory is transferred to permanent storage, which involves changes in the amount and composition of the molecules of ribonucleic acid (RNA) in the brain cells. Senile amnesia may be explicable on the grounds that the brains of elderly people are less well able to form RNA molecules.

2. *Proactive inhibition.* In this case the interference comes from what we read before reading the item we failed to recall. For example, our inability to remember the content of a chapter from a history textbook may be determined by the fact that before reading it we have read material of another kind.

This illustrates the fact that forgetting is a process of mutual interference or inhibition among the various items of information that have accumulated in our minds as a result of our reading.

Proactive inhibition, too, affects all three levels of the remembering process. It prevents us from memorizing properly; it prevents us from retaining properly, and it also prevents us from recalling properly.

One of the commonest sources of proactive inhibition is emotional in nature. Interference by inner emotional conflicts is apt to be a prime cause of forgetting the material we read. It affects our capacity to register what we see on the printed page. Not registering it properly, we are unable to recall it properly. 'Emotion,' said Dr Janet, 'makes people absent-minded.'

For example, a university student, a young woman of eighteen, found that both her concentration and ability to recall were poor. She was the only child of parents who engaged in frequent quarrels. In these quarrels she was forced to take sides. At home she had favoured her father but on going up to the university she felt herself to be on the side of her mother, who had been of brilliant intellectual achievement. Unable to tolerate this identification with her mother, which clashed with her sense of loyalty to her father, she found her studies interfered with by a severe mental conflict. A state of affairs, the seeds of which had existed in her home background *before* she went up to the university, was responsible for her poor concentration, memorizing and recall. She was a victim of proactive inhibition.

3. *Lack of attention.* Lack of attention causes an experience to make a weak impression on us, and this is another common reason why we forget. A poor memory is caused by not properly attending to what we wish to learn, so that it does not register with us strongly enough to remember it.

For example, suppose you are reading a book when someone asks you a question. To avoid being thought impolite you feel obliged to listen so that you can answer. But this act distracts your attention from your reading, so that you don't take in what you read. You are obliged to go back over the sentence or paragraph when you are once again free to attend to it.

I suppose one might argue that the fact that you heard the question at all is evidence that you were not properly attending to your book in the first place. This may well be true, illustrating how easy it is to deceive ourselves into thinking that we are attending when we are not really doing so.

4. *Insufficient repetition.* A poor memory is also caused by not repeating the material to keep it fresh in mind – by allowing time to elapse without refreshing the memory of what we have read. The more frequently the experience is brought to mind, the more firmly established the circuit its memory trace develops in the brain. Such memories may often persist for a whole lifetime.

Since our earliest schooldays we have all been familiar with the effect of repetition on learning. Ebbinghaus, the pioneer experimentalist in the field of memory, showed that if a series of syllables is learned until it can be repeated without a single mistake, fewer repetitions are required on the following day to achieve the same degree of learning. Moreover, the saving in time increases with subsequent repetitions and can be plotted graphically in the form of the well-known 'curve of learning'.

Much of what we know was acquired by this method of learning. We simply repeated it time and time again until we made it our own. We remember many of the details of our work in this way. We can go through them without hesitation because we have learned them thoroughly by carrying them out each day.

5. *Lack of interest.* Not being sufficiently interested in what we read is yet another reason why we may fail to remember it when we want to. The extent to which memory depends upon interest is illustrated by the following experience.

A young man said: 'I have met with a practical difficulty in remembering what I read faster. For example, if I tell myself that I have to remember some Spanish vocabulary, I am liable to forget the words unless they are extremely easy and I think about them frequently. I realize that it is to a certain extent a matter of interest, and that if one really wants to remember something important one can do so.'

The above person's experience also illustrated the part which attention plays in memory, for he added: 'I am particularly liable to forget if something unexpected happens to take my attention away from what I am trying to recall.'

'We remember best the things that interest us most,' writes Lionel Stebbing. 'If we can become really interested in a new fact ... we shall more easily remember it.'

6. *Inadequate associations.* Here we mean our failure to associate or mentally link up what we read with things we know already. This is a further cause of forgetting. Failure to form associations between new and old accounts for a poor memory of the contents of the printed page.

For example, a university student made some notes summarizing the thought content of Book V of Lucretius's poem *De Rerum Natura.* He noted Lucretius's argument that the gods did not create the world for the benefit of man. The following five considerations are adduced in support of this argument:

(a) Being blessed already the gods had no need of the gratitude of man.

(b) They needed to create the world neither for the sake of novelty nor to be cheered by the presence of human beings.

(c) It would not have hurt us not to have been born at all.

(d) The gods could not have created the world for men, for they had no model to guide them in forming an environment suited to human life.

(e) The world is full of imperfections which are inconsistent with divine perfection.

In spite of the methodical way in which the student arranged these ideas in his notebook he failed to remember them satisfactorily. This was because he omitted to associate them properly with other ideas already present in his mind. How he might have succeeded better will be discussed later in the chapter.

7. *Repression.* There is also a method of active forgetting of painful memories which is known as 'repression'. What happens in this case is that our interests, which, as we have seen, help to determine what we remember or forget, are bound up with our self-esteem. We more easily forget a memory which tends to conflict with our self-esteem than one which has not this tendency.

For example, a man said: 'If ever I persuade myself to read a horror story I forget it in case it comes back to haunt my sleep as a nightmare. I find later that I cannot recall even the broadest outline of what the story was about.'

The method of forgetting by repression is not under the conscious control of our will; it is rather a process which occurs without our being aware of it. Even if it were under conscious control, it could not be recommended for disposing of unpleasant memories, since it is apt to lead to the appearance of nervous symptoms.

We leave on one side a cause of forgetting which operates in the very young or the very old. This is the fact that the brain cells in which memories are recorded have not yet matured or have begun to deteriorate. In the former case it is not necessary to do anything about this, since young babies do not read and nature will take care of the matter anyway. In the latter case it is not possible to do anything about it even if we wished to. Senile amnesia is not remediable by any known medical means at the present time.

Memory and brain damage

Impairment of memory may also result from destruction of brain cells due to disease or accident. For example, a man of thirty said: 'I had cerebral meningitis when I was eleven years old, and three years ago I had a very serious motor-cycle accident in which I fractured my skull.' He complained: 'I wish I could remember more of what I read. My memory is not as good as I should like it to be.'

In such a case, of course, the remedy, where a remedy is possible, is a medical or surgical rather than a psychological one. Nevertheless one feels that even such a person might very well benefit to some extent by applying the methods of memorizing which will be discussed below.

What, then, are the implications of these findings from the point of view of improving our memory for what we learn to read faster? How can the seven basic causes of forgetting which were described above be overcome?

Forgetting: Cure

1. *How to avoid retroactive inhibition*. This means that we forget an impression because of other impressions which have followed it. We cannot eliminate this cause entirely but to reduce it can observe a period of rest after learning something. If we go on immediately to something else, what we have just learned may be forgotten.

In dealing with both this and the second cause of forgetting the general idea is to adopt methods of study which reduce interference from these causes.

After the rest period it may be advantageous briefly to go over the material again, revising what has already been read, so preventing it from passing out of mind altogether. Much of what we learn is forgotten almost as soon as we have learned it. We forget most rapidly immediately after learning and less rapidly as time goes on. This means that revision is most economical when carried out as soon as possible, subject to the provision that we give ourselves the rest period that will reduce interference, instead of immediately turning our attention to something new. For example, go over something again in the evening after learning it during the day.

'In general,' says D.O. Lyon, 'it was found that the most economical method for keeping material once memorized from disappearing, was to review the material whenever it started to "fade" ... The student is advised to review his "lecture notes" shortly after taking them, and if possible, to review them again the evening of the same day. Then the lapse of a week or two does not make so much difference. When once he has forgotten so much that the various associations originally made have vanished, a considerable portion of the material is irretrievably lost.'

2. *How to avoid proactive inhibition.* This means that something is forgotten because of the impressions we have before reading it. We tend to forget what we have read faster because of all the other things we have read and done before.

This cause of forgetting is obviously more difficult to control. However, we might benefit by taking a brief rest *before* we work on the practice material provided in this book. Essentially this is the same principle as the preceding one. It emphasizes the fact that work should be interspersed with rest periods if we are to get the maximum benefit from what we read faster in terms of remembering it better.

Another practical application of this principle is that the student should settle any emotional problems he may have before he attempts to commit his study material to memory. Then he can be sure that he has reduced a common source of interference from proactive inhibition which contributes to the likelihood of his forgetting what he plans to read faster.

3. *Pay attention.* To improve your memory pay close attention to what you wish to remember. To secure a strong impression of the material it is necessary to concentrate on it. The more vivid the impression the better it is recalled. Deal with the worries that distract attention from what you are trying to remember.

The importance of attention was amusingly illustrated in a strip cartoon which appeared in a newspaper. A man and his wife are seen setting off on a motoring holiday. He asks her whether she is sure that she hasn't forgotten anything. Has she stopped the milk and the papers? Turned off the water and electricity? His attention has been so occupied with what his wife might have forgotten that he himself has completely forgotten to fill up the car with petrol.

As the American psychologist W.B. Pillsbury put it, 'The key to the effectiveness of the process (of memory) ... is to be found in attention.'

Pay careful attention both at the time the impression is first received and at the time of trying to reproduce or recall it later.

'It is commonly recognized,' writes Dr William E. Galt, 'that unnoticed events cannot be reproduced, that attention to the stimulus is the essential condition for its later recall, and that the effectiveness of retention reflects the degree of attention during the registration of the impression. Furthermore, at the time of reproduction attention selects which of the many possible associates of a previous impression shall become effective.'

The reader is recommended to refer back to Chapter 2 for further advice on the problem of sustaining attention or concentrating.

4. *Repeat the material.* We must repeat whatever we wish to remember. We must repeat the material until we know it really well, revising it regularly to keep it fresh in mind.

However, repetition takes up time, which we are trying to save by learning to read faster. Therefore, we must ask: In what circumstances can repetition be reduced to a minimum and so allow us to save time on remembering as well as on reading? There is little point in reading faster if we are going to spend more time on memorizing by repetition.

This question is answered by Dr Bruno Furst and Lotte Furst, who point out that associations which are exaggerated or bizarre, or which involve movement, are apt to be remembered better than commonplace ones composed of static images. For example, a medical student who was concerned with the problem of remembering his textbook material said: 'I pick a patient or a friend and build the description of a disease around him. I place this person in a familiar room, garden or ward and I imagine these abstract things happening to him. I also think of things happening to him in time (that takes care of the *progress* of the disease).

'It is really fantastic how much can be crammed in and *remembered without revision*. Now I just store away facts and face the finals with optimism.'

This experience illustrates the point that if we follow Dr Furst's advice, it gives us a chance of reducing the number of repetitions necessary to remember what we read faster.

5. *Be interested in the material.* Have an interest in the thing you wish to remember. If your interest is weak or lacking altogether, you can strengthen or cultivate it in several ways.

One is to use auto-suggestion. You can strengthen your interest in the subject by suggesting to yourself: 'This interests me and I'll remember it' or 'This work is interesting me more and more' or 'This is useful to me and I like it better every day.'

Another is to read subjects allied to the one which you ought to interest yourself in. Such study may bring out more adequately the usefulness of the subject or show more clearly its relevance to contemporary events, thus stimulating your interest in it.

Thirdly, it is helpful to try to apply the subject to your daily affairs. Put what you wish to remember to some practical use.

Again, you can stimulate your interest by discussing the subject with someone – preferably with someone who knows more about it than you do. Such a person may be in a position to reveal to you the interesting facets of the topic, and to help you to gain an insight into and understanding of it which at present you lack. This insight and understanding may well help to stimulate not only your interest but also your memory. Always try to understand what you wish to remember.

Finally, you can stimulate your interest by giving yourself an incentive. Think of what you stand to gain by mastering the subject and of what you stand to lose by not mastering it.

The law of interest states that the greater the interest the fewer the repetitions required. If you are not interested in a subject, you can either give up studying it, or, if that is not practicable, develop an interest by any of the methods mentioned above.

6. *Form strong associations.* By association is meant the tendency of the mind to link impressions with other impressions already in the mind. Associate what you wish to remember with what you already know. You can remember the one by noting how it resembles the other, how it contrasts with it, or how it has in the past occurred together with it in space or time.

For example, take the case of the university student whose

efforts to remember the philosophy of Lucretius were referred to earlier in the chapter. He would have succeeded better had he taken the opportunity to compare Lucretius's views with those of the Christian religion, with which the student was already familiar.

The Christian view is that man is made in the image of God to enjoy the earth and to use its resources in the service of his Creator. The ideas of the Christian religion help one to remember by contrast the pre-Christian ideas of Lucretius. In particular, the last point in the argument is that the world is full of imperfections. This may be compared with other forms of philosophy, e.g., Christian Science, which deny the real existence of imperfections, attributing their apparent existence to errors of thinking on man's part. Such comparison and contrast are simple instances of the value of associating what we learn with what we know already.

Here is another example. Suppose we are reading some French vocabulary with a view to learning it and are required to learn that *la maison* = the house. We have to associate the new word with a word which we already know. We can do so through an intermediate linking word. For instance, we might drop the word 'mansion' or 'mason' or 'manse' in between the two in order to associate the French word with its English equivalent. Any of these words is chosen because they all resemble the French word in spelling and the English word in meaning.

Woodworth and Schlosberg have classified associations into four types. The first depends upon definition or connection, e.g., 'afraid' is associated with 'scared', 'table' with 'furniture', 'fish' with 'fin'. The second type depends upon description or function, e.g., 'afraid' is also associated with 'dark', 'white' is associated with 'snow', 'table' with 'eat', and so on. Then there is a third type of associations between things or ideas which are opposites or equals, such as 'afraid' and 'brave', 'white' and 'black', 'table' and 'chair', etc. Finally, a fourth type depends on our own personal experiences, attitudes, values, or idiosyncrasies. These are the things or events which are linked in our own minds but not necessarily in the minds of other people.

7. *Dealing with repression*. To deal with this cause of forgetting we must prevent the repression forming or lift it after it has formed. Unfortunately this takes us rather far outside the scope of this book. Anyone who suspects that his forgetting is mainly due to this cause would be better advised to consult his doctor and obtain an opinion on the desirability of consulting a psychiatrist, psychotherapist or psycho-analyst.

The latter expert especially is concerned with the problem of raising repressions and so removing the neurotic symptoms which are a mark of the existence of repression. Usually in such cases the forgetfulness is not the only symptom which troubles the victim. If he seeks this kind of treatment he will probably need it for other and even more serious problems than difficulty in remembering the material which he reads.

Psycho-analysis is a highly technical procedure which is both costly and time-consuming. Here we are concerned with the less serious causes of forgetfulness, which can be quite conveniently dealt with by much simpler methods.

It is worth mentioning in passing that the method of negative practice or conscious attention, which we learned about in Chapter 3, can be applied equally well to the problem of improving our memory for the material which we read faster.

In this case what is required is that instead of trying to remember we should try *not* to remember. For example, a name or a piece of information can be remembered by trying not to think of it at the same time as you imagine that you will.

This involves invoking the law of reversed effort, about which we also learned in Chapters 2 and 3. This law, we recall, states that in a conflict between will and imagination the latter proves the stronger. By an effort of will we try not to remember. At the same time we imagine that we shall remember. In this conflict imagination proves the stronger with the result that we actually do remember in spite of trying not to.

Summary
Now to summarize the contents of this chapter. The main causes of forgetting are seen to be as follows:

1. Interference from retroactive and proactive inhibition.
2. Lack of attention.
3. Insufficient repetition.
4. Lack of interest.
5. Inadequate associations.

To improve our memory for what we read faster we must tackle these basic causes of forgetfulness. In other words, training the memory depends upon avoiding interference, paying proper attention, repeating the material, being interested in it, and forming associations between it and what we already know.

SELF-TESTING QUIZ

Put a tick opposite the statements which you have read in Chapter 10.

1. Recording, retaining and recalling are the three R's of memory.
2. There is an easy way of improving the brain's power of retention.
3. We forget something because something else interferes with it.
4. Emotional conflict has no effect upon our capacity to register what we read.
5. A poor memory is caused by not properly attending to what we wish to learn.
6. Forgetting by repression is under the conscious control of the will.
7. Senile amnesia is remediable.
8. Disease or accident is never a cause of impairment of memory.
9. Go over something again in the evening after learning it during the day.
10. There is no need to intersperse work with rest periods.
11. The more vivid the impression the better it is recalled.
12. Tediousness is traditionally associated with the method of repetition.
13. Anything can be remembered whether you have any interest in it or not.
14. Never try to understand what you wish to remember – just remember it.
15. Associate what you wish to remember with what you already know.

Now check your answers against the answer key which you will find on page 159.

ANSWER KEYS TO SELF-TESTING QUIZZES
The statements which you should have ticked are listed below. If you have failed to tick any of them or have ticked any in addition to them your comprehension is less than perfect. In either case you should note your errors and refer back to the appropriate chapter, finding and underlining the correct versions of the statements which you were not sure about.

CHAPTER 1
WHY READ FASTER?
1, 2, 5, 6, 9, 11, 13, 14, 15.

CHAPTER 2
HOW TO CONCENTRATE
1, 4, 6, 7, 9, 12, 13.

CHAPTER 3
HOW TO READ FASTER BY NOT TRYING
1, 3, 4, 7, 9, 10.

CHAPTER 4
YOU CAN READ FASTER IF YOU KNOW MORE WORDS
1, 4, 5, 6, 8, 9, 10, 11, 13, 15.

CHAPTER 5
THE LINE AND CARD TECHNIQUES
1, 2, 7, 8, 9, 11, 13, 15.

CHAPTER 6
THE PENCIL AND TWO-LINE TECHNIQUES
1, 2, 3, 5, 7, 8.

CHAPTER 7
BEAT THE CLOCK AND GET THE IDEA
4, 6, 7, 8, 13.

CHAPTER 8
A CHANGE OF PACE IS AS GOOD AS A REST
2, 3, 5, 6, 7, 9.

CHAPTER 9
PRACTICE MATERIALS – IX-XII
2 (or 3 or 4), 7 (or 6), 10 (or 9), 13 (or 12 or 14 or 15).
In this quiz the following should be noted:
If you have ticked 1 you will probably have ticked 11 or 12. In this case you will find it advantageous to work through Chapters 5-8

again. If you have ticked 5 and have also ticked 2 or 3 or 4 you need to pay more attention to understanding what you read. This also applies if you have ticked 8. A positive answer to 2 or 3 or 4 together with 7 indicates a good standard of both speed and comprehension. In this case you will probably also have ticked 13 or 14 or 15.

CHAPTER 10
HOW TO REMEMBER WHAT YOU READ FASTER
1, 3, 5, 9, 11, 12, 15.

COMPREHENSION TESTS SCORE CHART

Enter up this chart as you complete each comprehension test. It will enable you to satisfy yourself that your comprehension need not suffer when you read faster. Indeed you may well find, especially as you get towards the end of the book, that you are understanding the material even better in spite of reading it faster.

SCORE	An Experiment in Education (Chapter 5)	Ancient Light on Modern Problems (Chapter 5)	The Man Who Disturbed the Sleep of the World (Chapter 6)	Child Guidance Report (Chapter 6)	Nouns in the Plural (Chapter 7)	Do We Live Hereafter? (Chapter 8)	Soviet Scientific Research (Chapter 8)	Practice Materials – IX-XII (Chapter 9)
100								
90								
80								
70								
60								
50								
40								
30								
20								
10								

Mark a cross in the appropriate box in each column.